CROSSCURRENTS *Modern Critiques*

CROSSCURRENTS *Modern Critiques*
Harry T. Moore, *General Editor*

Jac Tharpe

Nathaniel Hawthorne

IDENTITY AND KNOWLEDGE

WITH A PREFACE BY
Harry T. Moore

Carbondale and Edwardsville

SOUTHERN ILLINOIS UNIVERSITY PRESS

FEFFER & SIMONS, INC.

London and Amsterdam

To Prince Hal

JAC THARPE'S QUEST after identity and knowledge in Nathaniel Hawthorne has taken him on an interesting journey during which he has made some rewarding discoveries.

One of his points is that Hawthorne is not an exclusively American figure, a mutation out of puritanism. Mr. Tharpe is interested in showing that, whether or not Hawthorne had been influenced by certain European authors, he at least thought along the same lines as they did; and in turn he became an influence upon others. Mr. Tharpe believes that Hawthorne was bound to have been influenced by Goethe, but that Hawthorne may himself have influenced Dostoevsky.

In relation to one of Hawthorne's best-known stories, Randall Stewart has found traces of Spenser's The Faerie Queene; Mr. Tharpe hazards a further guess: " 'Rappaccini's Daughter' has several resemblances to Kalidasa's Shakuntala, which Thoreau read and might have recommended to Hawthorne"—a reasonable enough guess, too.

As Mr. Tharpe points out, "American criticism has been insular if not chauvinistic," though others have of course also noted similarities between Hawthorne and European authors. Perhaps the first to do so was Edgar Allan Poe, who in an 1847 review of one of the editions of Twice-Told Tales noted a resemblance to the German author Johann Ludwig Tieck: "Those who speak of [Hawthorne] as original mean nothing more than that he differs in his manner or tone, and in his choice of subjects, from any author of their acquaintance—their acquaintance not extending to the German Tieck, whose manner, in some of his works, is absolutely identical to that habitual to Hawthorne." But what Poe found disappointing in Hawthorne, Mr. Tharpe would see as valuable: a possible resemblance to Tieck makes Hawthorne all the less a parochial figure.

Mr. Tharpe also finds Hawthorne, somewhat in the manner of Laurence Sterne and Jane Austen, prefiguring the stream-of-consciousness writing of the twentieth century. Mr. Tharpe also makes out a good case for considering the posthumously published, incomplete Septimius Felton as perhaps a very early work. But perhaps his book's most helpful insight into Hawthorne is bound up with the ideas of identity and knowledge: what Mr. Tharpe calls violation, and by which he means the violation of another's individuality—probably, as Mr. Tharpe interprets it, what Hawthorne regarded as "the unpardonable sin." And this is in some ways like the discovery, by Osborn Andreas, of the "emotional cannibalism" in the fiction of Henry James—to James likewise an unpardonable sin.

There are many such insights and observations in this useful book. Its reader will find new perspectives throughout these continually rewarding pages.

HARRY T. MOORE

Southern Illinois University
February 22, 1967

ACKNOWLEDGMENTS

MOST OF THE FOLLOWING material was composed when I had access to little more of pertinence than a copy of the Riverside Edition of Hawthorne's work. Since then, it has become evident that a debt might have been due to numerous persons for insights and anticipations. But to record these in a set of notes at this point would be as equivocal as to claim originality. The bibliography is selected to include much of the important material, within the terms set forth in the headnote there. George E. Woodberry's book on Hawthorne is not mentioned nearly so often as it should be, and I should like to point to it specifically. Professors Harry Levin and H. C. Martin were consistently both charitable and helpful. Mr. Dean Fales and the Essex Institute have been consistently generous in diverse ways, and specifically in allowing use of the photograph of the painting of Hawthorne. Two student assistants, Larry Burk and William Matter, have been helpful with bibliography and quotations. Mr. Edward Fidel, a student assistant in the library, helped at a very important moment. And I should like to thank John Durand for a suggestion made long ago. The ideas of a great many students of Hawthorne may have gone into this revision, but they are too subtly influential to be clearly recognizable except as noted.

J. T.

CONTENTS

Nathaniel Hawthorne

IDENTITY AND KNOWLEDGE

1   THE CONTEXT

NATHANIEL HAWTHORNE's work needs reinterpretation, and it needs to be seen in the context of Western literature. American criticism has been insular if not chauvinistic. The sources of Hawthorne's ideas have in general been confined to the obvious or to the titles on the list [1] of books that were borrowed from the Athaeneum, which includes Theophilus Cibber but not either Shakespeare or Spenser among many others known to Hawthorne. This procedure gives the impression that Hawthorne's curiosity was confined to a few of the major figures of the Renaissance and his knowledge to that of early American history. If he was aware of figures closer to him in time, they were apparently Walter Scott and William Godwin. Even the possibility that Hawthorne's knowledge of the Renaissance was one source of his Gothicism is neglected for the more obvious conclusion that he depended on the Gothic novel. He is apparently thought to have been so isolated from the intellectual enthusiasms of his lifetime that he knew little or nothing of what went on around him. It may be true that Hawthorne was limited in this manner, but a likelier conclusion is that he tried to avoid or conceal the influences when he was aware of them. And if he really was isolated, he proves the greater for the fact that he was aware of so much without being informed from the outside.

Similar limitations have been placed on the potential of Hawthorne's influence, whether intentionally or not.

There is yet no study of Hawthorne and Eugene O'Neill or of Hawthorne's relationship to the neo-Gothicists of the South. The few studies of Hawthorne's possible influence on Henry James have indicated that more work should be done, and the same is true of studies of the relationship between the works of Hawthorne and William Faulkner. The general limits on both Hawthorne's sources and his influence could probably be imaginatively extended, even if there is little proof, with no more distortion than is now involved in estimates of Hawthorne's knowledge and experience.

The account of Hawthorne's relationship to German literature might turn out to be fascinating. He would have had an intuitive knowledge of the Faustian hero or a knowledge deriving from English sources, but of course it is inconceivable that he did not know J. W. Goethe's work when every intellectual of any stature in New England knew it. A reading of *Wilhelm Meister's Apprenticeship* turns up suggestions of parallels far too numerous to be accidental, one or two of which are mentioned in the text that follows. There is a pleasant enigma in the comparison of Hawthorne's early sketches with Heinrich Heine's early work, which apparently could not have been available to Hawthorne before he wrote the sketches. Hawthorne did know about Adalbert Chamisso's *Peter Schlemihl*, however, and had been enough interested in German literature to try to learn the language.

Surely, with an ability to read French, Hawthorne had a greater familiarity with French literature than is at once evident. He certainly knew Alain LeSage's *Gil Blas de Santillane*, which he mentions both in his own early picaresque sketches and in describing Holgrave in *The House of the Seven Gables*. Régis Michaud suggests [2] that there may be hints of *Tartuffe* in the characterization of Dimmesdale. Molière was probably as influential as Ben Jonson in conveying to Hawthorne an acquaintance with the "humour" tradition in the comedy of manners. In addition, possible echoes of the *Misanthrope* occur in, for example, the character of Roderick Elliston of "Egotism; or, the Bosom Serpent."

Yet more fascinating ideas derive from parallels between Hawthorne and figures whom he obviously did not
know. One of these was the German dramatist, Georg
Büchner, Hawthorne's contemporary, whose work was but
recently discovered. Büchner's frenzied Woyzeck might
have been one of Hawthorne's heroes. Hawthorne and
Büchner are both heirs to the Germanic *Drang* and to the
Norse myth of the twilight of the gods; they both realized
the value of the grotesque—and the useless. This appreciation of the transcendental grotesque, an outlook that either questions or ignores so much of traditional thinking,
derived from an acute consciousness in both writers of the
Dionysiac in both its Greek and its German forms.
Charles Baudelaire was a contemporary who had as little
success as Hawthorne in solving the various enigmas about
human worth, and he shares Hawthorne's pessimism.
Whether or not F. M. Dostoevsky was influenced by
Hawthorne, he is an example of another roughly contem-
poraneous figure who shows a close affinity with
Hawthorne's thought. Two articles [3] have been done on
this subject, but a great deal more could be said in an
analysis of the parallel ideas on human origins, motives,
actions and purpose, on psychological insight, on reform
and its relationship to human nature, and on the idea of
the underground man.

Hawthorne's influence abroad is another problem. In
great part, the influence may be indirect, a matter of
anticipations of themes. "The Artist of the Beautiful" is
only one example of Hawthorne's use of the theme of the
bourgeois and the bohemian that Thomas Mann later
explored so frequently, though of course Mann knew the
theme in Goethe. Franz Kafka's world of the haunted
dream was familiar to Hawthorne long before Kafka's
work was begun. So were Kafka's characters and settings
and his heroes, who wandered through shadows and ambiguities never to reach a goal. The relief in death felt by the
hero of *The Trial* is specifically Hawthornesque. Robert
Musil probably knew the work of Hawthorne, and there is
a potential study in determining the result. The suggestion was made above that a Germanic *Weltschmerz* in

Hawthorne might have made him intuitively aware of German themes, of Goethe's ideas for the tragic Faust or of Novalis' longing for death. Thus, of course, themes used by recent German writers need not have derived from Hawthorne. But as Andrew Schiller points out,[4] critics did not learn to read Hawthorne until after reading Kafka and James Joyce. Then, somehow, they almost forgot that Hawthorne came first. Thus, despite his real isolation and the theorizing about it, Hawthorne is in the Western literary tradition, picking up themes, creating in his own manner, and conveying themes to the continuing tradition.

The following essays deal with what may roughly be called the themes of seeing and being in Hawthorne's work. The title of the book presents these ideas as knowledge and identity. Seeing refers to observation and to the mental processes, such as cognition and reasoning, that follow observation. Being refers to human existence and to the enigmas regarding its source, specifically to the essence that may be related to being, either preceding or deriving from it. The enigmas make being itself the more mysterious. Thus, any one person is a miracle and a mystery. Hawthorne apparently was very much aware of the problems and of the unlikelihood of their being solved. For him, then, particularly in view of his knowledge of Puritanism, human motives and human acts were fascinating and quite as enigmatic as being itself. In having these interests, Hawthorne anticipates the widespread speculation about being that has arisen in recent years following the development of psychology and the decline of moral codes. The peculiar modernity of Hawthorne's work is gradually revealed in the following pages. It may be of some interest now to place the two major themes in the context of Western literature before continuing the discussion of Hawthorne's methods.

One or two quotations from the *Odyssey* will suggest the traditional framework of the theme for Western literature. When Odysseus arrives at the court of Alcinoüs wearing the clothes given him by Nausicaä, Arete the queen says,

Friend, I, for one, have certain questions for you.
Who are you, and who has given you this clothing? [5]

Conventional as the question may have been among relatively isolated peoples, it takes on a significance of some depth when Penelope later inquires the identity of the disguised Odysseus.

Friend, let me ask you first of all:
Who are you, where do you come from, of what nation
and parents were you born? [6]

Odysseus replies with flattery and deceit, perhaps with playfulness, and withal apparent sincerity.

O my dear lady . . . let it suffice to ask me
of other matters—not my blood, my homeland.
Do not enforce me to recall my pain.
My heart is sore; but I must not be found
sitting in tears here, in another's house:
it is not well forever to be grieving. [7]

Distant though they may seem, these references introduce precisely the topics that concern Hawthorne. The following pages will indicate that by the time he began to write the novels, every major character had to reply to the question of Arete and Penelope. Hawthorne also takes up the theme of clothing disguise and that of home, of which Odysseus appears to speak sincerely. The theme of home will, however, have ironic applications in Hawthorne's work. And most of Hawthorne's characters will be "forever grieving."

Themes of seeing and being are most elaborately handled in Western literature in Sophocles's *Oedipus the King*. Hawthorne's reflections upon identity and knowledge seem like brilliant elaborations of the *Oedipus*, though with deep insights that anticipate more recent speculation. *Oedipus* may have been the source of the idea for mystery plots that Hawthorne frequently uses. In any case, it presents for Western literature a second major document of the themes Hawthorne used. Oedipus in the fullest sense searches for his origins, for his home and his father, only to be left utterly homeless at the end of the action, destroyed by the replies to his questions. The figure of Tiresias is the focus for a good deal of linguistic and conceptual play regarding knowledge, on the serious levels from simple observation through reasoning to prophecy. The riddle of the Sphinx deals with the very important question of what man is.

Closer to Hawthorne chronologically is John Milton's treatment of seeing in *Samson Agonistes*, with its hero whose eyes are blind when the action begins and who therefore perceives by other methods. Significantly, despite a familiarity with *Paradise Lost*, Hawthorne does not use the mythology of the Christian faith within which Samson exists and performs. The Greek view in both the light and the dark aspects had more appeal to Hawthorne than the Christian view. Even when he uses certain of the Christian myths, which he took in part from Milton, he uses them for demonstrations that do not include hopefulness or salvation.

The nineteenth century itself, particularly in America, was concerned with identity and knowledge, in rather interesting variants of the older themes. In the numerous education novels of course the old theme continued. It is hardly an exaggeration to say that the question of individual identity was both universal and infinitely variable in art, particularly when Romanticism drew on. In addition, Romanticism emphasized diversity. So did Romanticism in America, where a land still widely unexplored continued to offer surprises in its flora and fauna, in its natural scenery and in its history. At Hawthorne's birth in 1804, the Lewis and Clark expedition was beginning, as a part of a general interest in nature that had been a part of the earlier Deist creed and that produced such books as William Bartram's *Travels through North and South Carolina, Georgia, East and West Florida* and Cadwallader Colden's *History of the Five Indian Nations of Canada*. Nineteenth-century America was thoroughly engaged in exploration and observation of diversity. Hawthorne's general relationship to this milieu has been discussed by James K. Folsom.[8] The milieu is reflected in Hawthorne's style, which is characterized by lists and catalogues of persons and objects. And Hawthorne's most frequent narrative mask was that of observer, of both the seen and the unseen. His cataloguing was in a sense an attempt to integrate seeing and being, to organize diversity by means of either perceived or fancied resemblances among individualities that would make them identifiable. And the context was in fact European. The tradition is that of Wordsworth who observed the common, and of Coleridge who observed the unusual; of Jonson who observed types of humanity; and of Chaucer, who observed what Hawthorne would have called "remarkables," and individualized types by the use of telling details. In France, Balzac and Zola also noted details and analyzed human types.

These observations suggest the general framework of the literary and thematic background of Hawthorne's work, all of which, however, was transformed by his peculiar view of things. The accounts are necessarily brief, for they are intended but to suggest the breadth of culture on which Hawthorne drew for his ideas. The real concern here is to perform a part of the task of reinterpretation. This intent requires a brief discussion of interpretations of Hawthorne.

In part as a result of the insular approach, criticism has tended to follow Henry James in extending patronage to Hawthorne. Hawthorne of course greatly annoys, with his moralization, his Gothic machinery, and his tendency to conceive all his stories as grandfather tales. Yet, most readers feel that despite these limitations, Hawthorne both displays strength and makes a subtle appeal to the perceptions. In the attempt to determine the source of this appeal, criticism has developed a few beliefs to attribute to Hawthorne. But these are characterized by a patronizing attempt to claim, by means of esoteric systematizing, that, despite Hawthorne's childishness and his paucity of ideas, he does have theories and doctrines like other artists. The search for doctrines is also an attempt to divest him of ambiguity, whereas, considering Hawthorne's philosophy, the ambiguous is the source of his strength, because it shows the nature of his insights and describes the world he perceived. Goodman Brown himself did not know what happened to him in the forest, thus suggesting that confusion is often the foremost result of experience.

The doctrines attributed to Hawthorne involve a head-heart psychology, isolation, an unpardonable sin, and a love for the hearth. Hawthorne is credited with a love of the public and a belief in universal depravity. He has, according to some, an optimistic spirit of democracy. He emphasizes feeling and denigrates intellect, particularly if it is inquisitive. He urges every man to find a place in the social order, and he disapproves of violation of the human psyche.

There is no doubt that these ideas appear in Hawthorne's work. And perhaps the frequent discussion of them indicates that most critics are dissatisfied with what has been said of them. But often the discussion is but repetition, and there is infrequent suggestion that the difficulty lies not in the interpretation of the ideas but in the importance given them. These few doctrines are characterized by the esoteric, the supernatural, or the archaic. There is appeal in relating art and the arcane, but the value of art is not in that relationship, nor is the value of criticism. Instead, the approach only raises a false body of knowledge to a level of appreciation.

These doctrines all need reconsideraton within a broader context, a context that in fact reveals Hawthorne to be a man of high literary excellence. The following essays assume the validity of Hawthorne's concept of violation of the individuality of another, and they examine some of the facets of the idea. The attempt is made, however, to show the relationship between violation and characterization and to show how both relate to the study of human nature. These concerns involve knowledge, the study of human origins and purpose, and the meaning of practical action. And these are more pressing matters than the vague concept of an unpardonable sin, which Hawthorne may not have taken at all seriously. The var-

ious other doctrines are examined below when they seem
appropriate, but they need thorough restudy, done with
the realization that Hawthorne had a sense of humor and
a sense of fantasy. He may have controlled neither sense
adequately in serious composition, but neither much de-
tracts from his appeal. And Hawthorne is certain to have
felt any strong conviction, even about violation or sin, to
be a cause of distortion in the personality. He was hesitant
to take any idea seriously and was never at ease with a
doctrine. On the one hand, he was too unsure and too
much afraid of being found out and embarrassed, like
Robin; on the other hand, he saw the distortion in others,
particularly in reformers and men of action.

Hawthorne's appeal derives from a mythmaking power
in general and from a philosophical approach to the study
of action, psychology, and being. He ponders what occupies all intellectuals and what always appeals to them, the
problems of origin and purpose, yet he is not so highly
speculative as Dostoevsky and is thus in a sense more
practical in his concerns. Hawthorne tends to write comedy of manners on the level of myth, creating, somewhat
like Friedrich Schiller's "naïve" poet, with an intuitive
awareness of the archetypal and the phylogenic. He anticipates much of the body of the English novel, and he
anticipates the French existentialist movement in many of
its concerns, particularly in his use of the isolated and
dispassionate stranger and in his portrayal of a bleak universe from which there is no exit.

Hawthorne himself was even more modern than his
work. His style, though graceful, has a touch of the antique, and he was charmed by oddities. His moralization,
though impish and conventional, seems at times intended.
These are distracting idiosyncrasies, but Hawthorne himself was thoroughly without illusion regarding the traditional methods and myths. He perceived in contraries and
paradoxes and had, consequently, a strong sense of the
absurd. Everything, for him, probably, was potentially
absurd, including himself. This awareness is not incompat-
ible with his characteristics of a strong pride, a gentle-

manly baring, a conventional morality, and a mind for practical affairs. The difficulty is that all these *may* exist together in a man, emphasizing his dissociation at least to himself, and making him appear to be two or even more persons. To alleviate this situation of awareness of the absurd and the concomitant realization that perhaps if one tried a little harder or knew a little more he could find the answers, Hawthorne drew upon a sense of humor. Such humor often, however, will reflect but the concealed grimaces of a man making a desperate attempt to achieve equanimity.

Hawthorne is persistently concerned with the problem of knowledge, particularly with regard to human action. He examines the question of right conduct, the relationship between characters and acts, the nature of personality and being, and the meaning and value of human action. He uses mystery plots in order to emphasize the problem, and he devises numerous situations in which one person exercises hidden influence on the actions of another. He creates situations in which one person is observed by others or in which members of a group observe one another. By these methods, he inquires far more persistently into the ways of fate and providence than do any of the scientists whom he sometimes, with tentative seriousness, castigates. The antithesis of ignorance and knowledge, vaguely symbolized by darkness and light, is a major theme in most of the great works. Tales of the supernatural and the psychological are attempts to divine and record some kind of knowledge. Hawthorne is a purveyor of secrets of the universe which are to be passed on to men. Milton stood as intercessor to justify God's ways to men. Hawthorne stands as a seer between men and the way of things. He claims little success in the attempt to elucidate, however, apparently concluding that certain knowledge is not to be had.

Thus, Hawthorne's speculation is limited in that it presupposes a pessimistic doubt that human action and human existence can be of value. He realized somewhat early in his career that he could not find any better solution for the mystery of life than he could for the mystery of himself, which was probably his first interest. The search was made with the realization that search is generally useless. There may be some bare chance that nature can, as he says in "The Haunted Mind," be caught off guard and made to reveal a secret, but one does not count on that. And despite occasional pious references to a creator, it is nature that Hawthorne challenges, not God; for there is but little indication that, except when he is self-conscious, which may be often enough, or when Hawthorne is simply using conventional terminology, he has any concern with traditional concepts of a god that is a personal, conscious deity. This approach derived in part from a courage that refused to blame the unknown for the plight of man, but it must also have derived from the recognition that if something existed with the power to make changes, improvement would long ago have been made.

If Hawthorne had a doctrine of knowledge or an epistemology, it was probably agnostic. He did not know, and he did not approve of those who did. Numerous perceptions of the apparently irrational led to thorough indecision. The ambiguity found in Hawthorne's style essentially characterizes the man. For him, there were always alternatives, though none led to decision or success. Eventually, he learned to amuse himself and tantalize others by combining the alternatives and creating ambiguity. But indecision in action, or agnosticism in everyday life, though perhaps the most logical position, is the most difficult to maintain. A man often forgets that he has no opinions or beliefs. Too, daily life sometimes requires him to act as if he had. When in doubt or under pressure, the agnostic, if he must act, would probably do so within the easiest framework, that of his upbringing, unbiased or varied as it may have been. Thus, Hawthorne may often reflect Puritan ethics, for example, without having any convictions about Puritan virtues. But he will be inconsistent. He may be transcendental, democratic, unitarian, aristocratic, and many other things, at some time. There may even be a pattern in the inconsistency, though it is doubtful that Hawthorne would have approved of the discovery of one. But lack of conviction explains the diversity of a man's actions and ideas, as Hawthorne realized. That is how in "Night Sketches" he can deny being a chameleon, though claiming to be sympathetic, and how Coverdale can insist on an individuality that he does not have while disapproving of those, like Hollingsworth and Zenobia, who are somewhat individualistic.

Even as a logical system, agnosticism is difficult to maintain. There is a paradox in that complete openmindedness should presume to construct a system. Yet one is not entirely able to live as a perpetual opportunist, devising successful methods of action at every moment. Some decisions must come from habit. The difficulty of the constant need to consider, deriving from the loss of illusions and the lack of assurance, is one of the reasons that the present time may be called the age of anxiety. Indecision will be easy for a very observant person, but agnosticism, the paradoxical formulation that he ought to follow, may be impossible. It may be indeed that a strong awareness of all these matters caused Hawthorne actually to conceive of agnosticism as some kind of ideal in every way, as a philosophy of life, and as a guide for action. This decision would help to explain the several indifferent and detached figures, such as Coverdale and Gervayse Hastings, who appear in his work. Being Hawthorne, suspicious of all systems, all doctrines, and all conclusions, he would never have been convinced about the validity of the agnostic ideal or any other, and this may explain why he sometimes chides himself or his characters for their coldness and indifference. These facets of Hawthorne, the diversity, the agnosticism, and the indifference in his characters, are, however, some of the reasons for his appeal. Such characteristics, in the man or in the fictional character, may not seem good, but they seem true, which is often the most that can be said about truth.

For many sincere intellectuals who have felt the necessity of giving up attempts to keep the first commandment, a tentative solution to the problem of the absurd and irrational is a practice of the second commandment: love one another. This solution reflects, however, a concerted attempt not to construct a philosophy of life but only to avoid despair, yet it leads to the codification of belief, as any doctrine will, which may in turn lead to another disillusionment. Hawthorne not only disapproved of beliefs and doctrines, but he also seems not to have found love to be a tenable solution to the human problem. He did have experience with the idea. But the *Blithedale Romance*, which records the actions and motives of a community of idealists and a brotherhood of men, reveals only distorted egoists with hidden, selfish motives. They are accurately portrayed as human, of course, and are to be hesitantly condemned. Coverdale, also human, makes some attempt to understand, but he shows no love or compassion and makes no suggestion that any hope lies in that course. It is true that Hawthorne writes a story in which love is urged as a cure for egoistic jealousy, but this story is so unconvincing as to appear false. Hawthorne may himself simply have been afraid or incapable of love. "Night Sketches" and *The Blithedale Romance*, which propose human sympathy, suggest that he tried to develop an ethics of compassion in his detachment, but that he was not successful, as Coverdale makes evident. The idea was in any case somewhat egoistic. Hawthorne was bound to realize eventually that he was not made to reveal the divine.

He moved gradually from the dubiously humble attempt at sympathetic observation to distinctly inquisitive observation, from the attempt to explain to the attempt merely to understand if possible. Love after all may be another illusion. The logical result of such a tenet is the idea of forgiving all. Hawthorne would perhaps not have rejected that ethic, or he might even have practiced it, but he would not necessarily have been convinced by it. One may forgive all yet disapprove of nearly all as being wrong action. The result of so much awareness almost has to be indifference, which appears to have been the result for Hawthorne, along with, however, a characteristic lack of conviction. When awareness is thorough, clear enough to show the pettiness of human beings, regardless of where the fault lies, compassion may derive only from timidity or hypocrisy.

Identity refers to the other aspect of the subject treated below. For the most part, it signifies ignorance. The word is intended to have among its connotations the Greek concept of knowing oneself. Associated is the journey theme, which frequently occurs in Hawthorne's rich and varied treatment of the subject. The journey is associated especially with such tales as "Young Goodman Brown" and "My Kinsman, Major Molyneux," but it appears also in the careers of Coverdale and Holgrave. Both in the early Oberon papers and much later, again with Holgrave and Coverdale, Hawthorne shows a hesitant interest in the picaresque, with its wandering hero.

More often, Hawthorne is concerned with what may be called by the cliché, the odyssey of life. The term of course derives from Homer's epic, and the connotations are intended specifically to include the account of the vicissitudes that occur during the lifetime of a man. The suggestion is certainly of a life of difficulties. Included too is the idea of erratic wandering with but a vague goal, if there is one at all. If home is the goal, as with Odysseus, the emphasis nevertheless is on the process, on the incidents, the adventures and the episodes that affect the character involved. In Hawthorne's work, the goal appears to be almost nonexistent; thus, there is a special emphasis on the process. The lack of a goal leaves little hope, and the lack of hope makes the wandering appear to avail nothing for Hawthorne's characters, whereas Odysseus was at least going home.

The subject of identity as discussed below refers, however, not only to the character's quest for self-knowledge but also to Hawthorne's effort to get knowledge about human identity—life, character, and being. He attempts to lay human existence completely bare, as in the figures of Goodman Brown and Hester Prynne. This theme appears with so much frequency and intensity that it integrates Hawthorne's work, and thereby suggests a need for reinterpretation. "Rappaccini's Daughter," for example, is reinterpreted below within the framework of these themes of ignorance and knowledge as applied to the enigma of being. Hawthorne's treatment of the problem of identity investigates not only the matter of self-knowledge, which is essentially Goodman Brown's problem, but also the matter of knowing others, which is a major theme of the *Scarlet Letter*, where it is pertinent to each of the four main characters. The breadth and detail of this concern will be seen below.

The complexity of the theme cannot be overemphasized, and the analysis of it is involved. The concern is with human motives and human action and with what an act may reveal of character, the problem that drives Giovanni mad. An act may reveal something about a person, but only if one knows that it is a characteristic action and that it is not acting. In addition, the character of the person who observes will affect his perception, as is also the case with Giovanni, whose lust influences him to perceive Beatrice as he wants her to be.

Hawthorne was never sure about these matters, because he saw a great many complexities. He follows Shakespeare and anticipates Dostoevsky in having so much awareness that he is confused. The knowledge and the confusion are expressed in some of the methods used to present the complexities of the problem he studied. Themes of disguise and the double are chief among them.

The theme of clothing as symbol and disguise, perhaps under the specific influence of Thomas Carlyle's *Sartor Resartus*, could be traced throughout American literature. It appears not only in Hawthorne and in Herman Melville's *White Jacket* and *Confidence Man*, but also in such diverse works as Mark Twain's *Huckleberry Finn* and James's *The Real Thing*. The theme symbolizes the search for identity. But while clothing may reveal, it may also deceive. Whether or not clothes make the man depends, as in the case of Feathertop and Judge Pyncheon, on whether one knows the man and the clothing. Clothing is, in short, recalling the Platonic hierarchy, another step removed from the ideal form of which man himself is but an imitation. The possibilities for symbolism in clothing are as numerous as the ambiguities in personality and action.

One must know how to read the symbols. In the *Blithedale Romance*, the participants wear similar work smocks, a practical usage which probably also symbolizes equality. But this disguise causes Westervelt to misapprehend Coverdale at their first meeting, which Coverdale, revealing incidentally how little he accepts the idea of equality, very much resents. The scene also reveals how Westervelt acts with a man in a workman's smock. Actions perhaps do reveal under some conditions. Westervelt, as Coverdale eventually learns, is but a scarecrow dressed in fine clothing, in this respect resembling both Feathertop and Judge Pyncheon. Feathertop, apart from the immediate comparison, is the symbol of all men, both in that they are men of straw and in that they are not entirely responsible for being so.

Hawthorne often associated a specific article of clothing or dress with a character. Besides Zenobia's exotic flower, there are more distinctly sartorial items like Hepzibah's turban and Clifford's faded dressing gown or Old Moodie's patch and Hester's scarlet embroidery. Purses are symbols of Priscilla, and Pearl's dress is in some way symbolic of her purpose, while the minister uses a black veil to symbolize the hidden portion of the self. On the other hand, Hepzibah's turban is but a symbol of her wish to be an oriental princess. Holgrave is delineated symbolically in the account of his various garbs as, like a (Victorian) picaro, he shifts professions in the gradual move toward the realization of himself. Old Moodie's former and latter states are contrasted in great part by descriptions of the differences in his clothing. Finally, in Hawthorne's various novel fragments, the lost heir to the English line disguises himself and is lost in the American wilderness.

Hawthorne's interest in the theme of identity is revealed also in the complex symbolism of names. In such figures as Old Moodie or Chillingworth, the use of false names would seem like a mere Gothicism. But in view of the frequency and variation of his use of the technique, Hawthorne must intend something more than oddity. Zenobia's name is never revealed. Holgrave's name conceals a Maule who would seem like a threat if he were known to the Pyncheons. Suggestive of greater seriousness, the hero of the novel fragments never learns his last name, and he also does not learn his origins. The name appears to symbolize the mystery of being in several ways, and the problem of names appears to be related to the problem of adjustment to the world. In general, Hawthorne's characters do not know themselves and are not known by others. On the other hand, a few, Donatello and Giovanni in particular, name themselves quite simply, without apparent question and for little apparent reason. Donatello may declare his innocence and simplicity in the statement, but in naming Miriam with as much naïveté he reveals ignorance of her complex being. Whatever Giovanni's naming of himself means, the meaning has to differ from that of Donatello. Dimmesdale and Hilda, though in different circumstances, yet perhaps for reasons not dissimilar, wish to confess without reserve. Different as their circumstances are, both wish to be known thoroughly. Hilda of course wants her purity established. Dimmesdale wants to be recognized as the sinner and to be reassured as to his worth. Both are egoistic. Hawthorne has intuited in these cases something fundamentally true about human psychology. In Dimmesdale's thinking, paradoxically, there is a probable wish for punishment, too, perhaps to the point of death. In the case of Mr. Hooper, the black veil effaces identity, in a rough parallel of Dimmesdale's wish. And both characters show variants of Hawthorne's recurrent theme, begun in *Fanshawe*, of the hero's voluntary withdrawal from any conflict of circumstances. Thus, in view of the elaborate diversity of Hawthorne's investigation of character and personality, the concern with names appears to be a serious use of symbolism in characterization. The man without a name has a search to make. The man with a concealed name is perhaps avoiding a search or avoiding knowledge of himself. And in a sense, the technique is another of Hawthorne's methods of creating the double that allows a man to view his other self.

These various symbols indicate the complexities that Hawthorne perceived in the study of human action as he dealt with the practical matter of characterization. But the intuition that much of the self was unknown led to a more elaborate symbol. Assuming that "Alice Doane's Appeal" was the first tale, Hawthorne shows an interest in the double from the beginning of his work. The figure appears thereafter in such variants as the fellow traveler in the picaresque tale called "Passages from a Relinquished Work" and as Robert Hagburn in *Septimius Felton*. Variants appear in "Monsieur du Miroir," in the devil-grand-father identification of "Young Goodman Brown," in the father-son identification of the novel fragments, and perhaps in "My Kinsman, Major Molyneux."

Ignorance in the search for the self creates the double, the shadow, the ancestor, the self of the dreams or the memories, the seeming, the other, what one was yesterday when he was simple and foolish, or what inconceivable personality he may have on another day when he has a moment of awareness. It also indicates the desire of the introvert and the sensitive, lonely person for a companion who will receive his confession and know him as well as he knows himself. Perhaps, if the analogy is illuminating, the desire should be stated in terms of the myth recorded in Plato of the individual's need to be round and whole. The suggestion is of a dream of being all that one is not, in terms of what one conceives of himself as being, from the child's wish to be an adult to the adult's wish to be the man of the advertisements. In its simplest form the double is the companion of one's dreams. The most complex of his forms is apt to be pathological.

"Alice Doane's Appeal" is Hawthorne's most intense and serious treatment of the theme. Even so early, the theme is related to the father-son identification that

Hawthorne used in the novel fragments. Other uses of the theme are somewhat more facetious and perhaps more healthy. If *Septimius Felton* was in conception really one of the later works, however, the theme remained in Hawthorne's mind throughout his career.

Hawthorne also uses the double or the Doppelgänger theme as a technique. Many of his works deal with the foil, suggesting that Hawthorne was aware from the beginning of Goethe's theme of the bohemian and the bourgeois. The awareness is reflected in Hawthorne's wish to be a writer in spite of the disapproval of the family, the townspeople of Salem, and the Puritan tradition. This debate, along with numerous others in Hawthorne's mind, must have led to the development of a perhaps unrecognized agnosticism and to a technique that used ambiguity with both seriousness and facetiousness in what he thought as well as what he wrote.

Hawthorne frequently uses the theme of one person's attempt to control another. Action on the wish to master the self creates and destroys, reforms and demands allegiance. Westervelt provides a superficial view of such a figure. Hollingsworth is a more realistic portrayal of one. Zenobia dominates Priscilla, and Old Moodie dominates them all. The theme motivates action in "Sylph Etherege," *The House of the Seven Gables, The Marble Faun,* and in most of Hawthorne's work.

It may or may not have been a combination of the impulse to find the self that led Hawthorne to write a few stories in which figures were actually created. "The Snow Image" and "Drowne's Wooden Image" seem far removed from what a young man does in projecting himself. Yet Drowne's image is, in the usual terms, his other, the woman of his dream, the anima and the other half of the round being of the Platonic myth. "Feathertop" deals with man in general and also with his creator, neither of them showing much dignity. Mother Rigby and Drowne are more fully sketched examples of the figure of the wise ambassador of the gods that Hawthorne uses at times, rather as Milton designates the angels to justify God's ways. There are differences. Hawthorne does not take on Milton's problem, nor does he have Milton's belief.

In view of these many complexities that prevented assurance and tired both body and soul of a man who very much wanted to know, it can be no surprise that a subtle consciousness of death pervades Hawthorne's view of life. Indeed, he shows an inclination to nihilism that precludes the development of a constructive philosophy of life. A pervasive concern with the search for identity and place indicates a desire for peace and for an end to all searching and striving. This is assumed and implied throughout the following essays. Hawthorne's Faustian characters appear in contexts that do not open with the "Prologue in Heaven," which means that the striving comes to no end. Hawthorne analyzed and described a world of dissociated and maladjusted persons like himself without having much sympathy for them and yet without blaming a higher being. He saw no way out, and the early and continuous impression of such a view developed, or intensified, in him a sorrowful enervation that made him wish for the ultimate and complete escape. He is not optimistic. Sometimes he is able to ignore the problem for awhile by forgetting the insights that encourage pessimism.

Home, a term discussed in some detail in the conclusion, appears to be for Hawthorne a symbol of a progression of concepts, roughly location, anonymity, and death, all of which are of such depth as to be associated with nonexistence—oblivion. The intention appears to be the avoidance of a continuous striving, of the expenditure of mental and physical energy under conditions that make human action, even when, on rare occasions, it can be sensibly interpreted, seem thoroughly useless. The extreme diversity of things and persons, a diversity that is, however, perhaps superficial, is confusing. As chapter 4 suggests, Hawthorne attempts to categorize as a way of handling the diversity. It seems likely that he eventually found the method to be in general but another distortion of such fact as may be apparent. But in this categorizing he apparently finds a method of operation, as another man might use a set of theological assumptions, or another relate his novels by making cross references to characters. Within the framework based on roughly-defined categories for the animate as well as the inanimate, Hawthorne proceeds to create and persistently use thereafter a limited number of types for his characterization. The types are used to illustrate the process toward death and the inclination toward oblivion. Home, thus, is a place of rest for all men and for all manner of men. Safely there, they are no longer involved with suffering. Obviously, therefore, the perfect home is oblivion. Possibly, the idea was forced upon Hawthorne by a cognizance of the inevitability of death. That is, if the end eventually is death, can there be any reason at all for suffering at length while moving toward the inevitable?

For Hawthorne there seems to have been a direct relationship between the human action he studied as a man and the characterization he attempted as a novelist, or between his philosophical speculation and his writing technique. The conclusion he came to was that character could not be known, which implies that human action is of no value. If human action is of no value, human beings are in a predicament, one for which, it would seem, they are not responsible. Yet, Hawthorne may not have been willing to exonerate them. If he did not blame them for their plight, he showed them feeling guilt for their actions and thus adding to their own troubles. They make things further difficult for themselves by setting up moral codes and ideals that involve what is called guilt or sin. But despite occasional remarks about love, Hawthorne appears to have felt little for his fellow men. Perhaps he sometimes unconsciously felt sympathetic with the outcasts, or at least understood them. Certainly, he has little sympathy for the constructivists and reformers.

Hawthorne is objectively concerned with observation and reflection, and he is more indifferent to theory and system than the search for doctrines recognizes. He asks life and nature the riddle of the Sphinx, and his work as a whole records the ambiguous, impassive, Sibylene reply that he receives in answer to his questions. For this analysis of human existence and human action, he needs moving figures, which he creates without much regard for characterization. He conceives of persons as phantoms of a haunted mind. Depending on the substance he allows them, according to whether they act in a story, a novel, or an allegory, they may be shadows, types, or representative figures. In the latter half of his career he concentrates on not types but examples of people, whom he inevitably finds enigmatic, usually distorted, and nearly always unhappy.

Despite Hawthorne's talk about not revealing himself, much of his work can be taken as remarkably detached autobiography. It seems likely that he was more than merely the two persons he is often said to have been. He was childlike and childish; sardonic, whimsical, and humorous; both shy and bold—and immensely sorrowful. He was reasonable and irrational. He was probably a perfectionist. And his obsession with reform probably means that he was a disillusioned idealist and reformer. In any case, when one examines Hawthorne's work as a whole, one concludes that Hawthorne was, even after his marriage, in no sense either adjusted or happy. A man of numerous moods and facets shows them all. But a happy man does not show so many unpleasant and unhappy figures in such unpleasant circumstances. Nor does a man of compassion appear so often indifferent. A man once capable of compassion may. If Hawthorne seems reasonable, it may be the result of his grudging realization that "Life is like that," not reasonable, indeed, but necessary. "Young Goodman Brown" is taken, herein, to be far more representative of Hawthorne's work and of the man himself than any story that displays blithe ingenuity.

DURING THE PERIOD before publication of *The Scarlet Letter*, Hawthorne experimented a good deal with first- and third-person narrators. The discussion of the topic is complicated from the very first by the fact that dates of publication for much of Hawthorne's work are not accurate indications of the dates of composition. The observation may hold true for more than the short stories and sketches. There is, for example, much in the tone and the themes of *Septimius Felton* to suggest that it was an early work and not a late one, at least in conception. One can only guess as to explanations, but there was so much tampering by the family and so much secrecy in Hawthorne himself that one need have no implicit trust in the usual chronology. There are many suspect details in Hawthorne's biography, such as the claim that he wrote the notebook passages as they stand, without ever revising. The *Blithedale Romance*, with its cranky first-person narrator, seems oddly placed after the *Scarlet Letter* and the *House of the Seven Gables*, for one who hopes to find any process of development in Hawthorne's work. The difficulty about dates and development means that in discussing the various masks and poses, one uses but a rough chronology based first on the general idea that the more mature followed the less mature. Even so, there are complexities, for in the midst of the various experiments with narrative masks, Hawthorne published highly competent third-person narratives, among which are "Young Goodman

Brown" and "My Kinsman, Major Molyneux." *Fanshawe,*
which was competent third-person narration, was *followed*
by the experimentation. Thus, one suggests for the most
part only that the experimentation with masks was the
result of indecision after the publication of *Fanshawe* and
that various masks were used at roughly the same time in
the period thereafter, before Hawthorne finally settled on
straightforward, third-person narrative as used in the novel
fragments and in the novels except the *Blithedale Romance.*

Fanshawe, though often deprecated by critics, is hardly
worse than many another man's first published novel. In
Hawthorne's case, the first novel is quite suggestive. There
is no assurance in speculating about Hawthorne's reasons
for destroying the novel after its publication, and the
discussion that follows will not be conclusive. The assumption usually is that he was ashamed of the work,
which may be the case. The author of "Young Goodman
Brown" and the artist who first conceived of "Alice
Doane's Appeal" might justly have been ashamed of *Fanshawe.* There is an interesting question, however, as to
whether it was the man Hawthorne and not the artist who
was ashamed of the novel. The young artist had no serious
reason to feel ashamed unless he wished at some point to
hide the situations and characters that recall the Gothic
novel and the influence of its authors. This appears to be
insufficient reason in view of Hawthorne's later Gothi-
cisms. In any case, the imitation of the Gothic novel has
concealed good touches. There are bits of realism, for
example, particularly in the characterization of the land-
lord. The characterization of Dr. Melmoth is done with a
pleasant sense of humor. Aside from these observations,
which, however, are not attempts to raise the stature of
Fanshawe, the authorial mask is of interest.

One would expect the author of a first novel to write
autobiographically, at least in sentiment. That is, he
would be likely to sympathize with any young man who
appeared in the action. Hawthorne obviously does sympathize with Fanshawe, but there are qualifications. The

sympathy is revealed in the action rather than in the style or tone, for the most part, that is in Fanshawe's acts rather than in the description of his thoughts. Hawthorne seems to have been aware of a need to restrain a youthful, naïve and personal intimacy with Fanshawe. Thus, Fanshawe shares the author's sympathy with Walcott, the double, the man whom the moody Fanshawe might have wished to be if he ever would have agreed to be anyone but himself. What happens is that Hawthorne begins in *Fanshawe* on a problem that continues to interest him throughout his career. This is the matter of the other self, and its several involvements with the questions of immortality and idealization. These combine to cause a sensitive young man to conceive of himself as a lamenting observer at his own death. Fanshawe is content to withdraw from the love intrigue because he really lives on as Walcott and thus has the best of both worlds. This theme has reverberations in Hawthorne's work that will be discussed in the next chapter.

The author's intimacy in this first novel is with neither of the men but with the heroine. As a later chapter points out in more detail, it is with Ellen that Hawthorne's description of thought approaches *style indirect libre*, a narrative technique that would have led to the psychological novel if Hawthorne had cared to use it. For reasons not determined, among which may be the wish to avoid or conceal autobiographical elements that might have been associated with the male characters, the author spends a good deal of time in recording Ellen's indecision and her impressions, as he does in Hilda's case much later. Perhaps he felt a need to show that Ellen was virtuous despite her actions, an approach that was used with Beatrice in "Rappaccini's Daughter." But in view of Hawthorne's wish for secrecy, as indicated by his actions and his various remarks about concealing himself, notably in "The Old Manse," it is possible that *Fanshawe* taught him a great deal about himself, once the urge to publish left him free to see the material somewhat objectively. In having the awareness to avoid the mistake of an immature sympathy with the male characters, he may have overlooked other mistakes. He was to return off and on to third-person narrative while developing masks that both concealed and revealed.

Much in *Septimius Felton* suggests that it was conceived soon after the publication of *Fanshawe*. If it was not, the following observations may be made of the end of Hawthorne's career as well as of the beginning. Thus, the matter of chronology, even of works that may be many years apart, does not affect the rest of the observations. One indication, however, that *Septimius Felton* is an early work is that the plot development resembles that of *Fanshawe*, as if Hawthorne wished to treat his original themes in another form. As in *Fanshawe*, the portion of *Septimius Felton* that presents Rose as the fiancée of Septimius gradually develops into a situation that prepares for the more energetic rival to be the young woman's husband. Hawthorne, apparently later, changed the plot to make Rose the sister of Septimius and to substitute for her the strange figure of Sibyl, either the first or the last of Hawthorne's enigmatic women. Thus again the figure of Ellen is removed from the more sensitive of the doubles. Septimius himself eventually withdraws to anonymity, in a move that parallels Fanshawe's willing death.

The differences between the two situations in *Fanshawe* and *Septimius Felton* are revealing. The basic plot is retained as noted, with the three characters and the girl as the object of interest to a very sensitive youth and to a rival with quite other sensibilities. The Gothic is hardly avoided; though, in *Septimius Felton*, Hawthorne is more inventive, perhaps under the influence of Charles Maturin's *Melmoth the Wanderer*. The differences center on characterization of all three figures. Walcott has become more dissociated from Fanshawe. Fanshawe is more secretive and morose, and Ellen, as Rose, is hardly the author's concern. Sibyl, the enigmatic sister of the simpler women in Hawthorne's work, has appropriated the author's curiosity. The question of immortality is not associated with the character and his double but is simply discussed by the hero and his dissociated foil. The idealization of himself that Fanshawe contemplates is reflected only in the simple wish that Septimius has for eternal youthful existence. The wish for the double and the interest in immortality remain, however, to turn up again in the Oberon papers.

The figure of the sensitive and youthful Oberon is usually considered to be Hawthorne's first pose after the third-person narrative of *Fanshawe*. This figure is evidently not a Fanshawe, though he may be implicit in the conception of Fanshawe. He is more like an intense and articulate Walcott, suggesting that Hawthorne did in fact conceive of himself as being both Fanshawe and Walcott. The theme of the double and that of the self viewing the other in some mental immortality arises again in the Oberon papers when the narrative of the distraught Oberon is told by a reasonable friend who is a prototype of the serene narrator of "Night Sketches" and "Footprints on the Sea-shore." Hawthorne seems to have been working under various influences in these early works, and the Oberon papers distinctly appear to result from a storm and stress period directly influenced by Goethe's *Wilhelm Meister*, and, from some distance, perhaps also by Goethe's earlier novel, *The Sorrows of Young Werther* and by Lord Byron's *Childe Harold*. *Childe Harold* would of course seem more likely, both because the work is English and because Byron's influence may appear in the experience of the sublime in nature that is recorded in "My Visit to Niagara." Yet the sentimental incident of Oberon's death seems Wertherian too, in view of the possible influence of *Wilhelm Meister* on "The Devil in Manuscript," another of the Oberon papers, and in other ways to be noted. Two episodes in the first book of *Wilhelm Meister* show Wilhelm and his friend Werner in scenes of manuscript burning. In the second particularly, Wilhelm becomes quite as distraught as Oberon. The difference is that Hawthorne's sense of humor intervenes, perhaps self-consciously, in reaction to Goethe's Wertherian sentimentality, and Hawthorne's account ends with a touch of the grotesque. A further suggestion of the influence of Goethe on these Oberon papers is that the theme of the bohemian and the bourgeois, later developed in "The Artist of the Beautiful," somewhat affects the characterization of the figures of Oberon and his friend respectively as it does the characterization of Wilhelm and Werner respectively.

Hawthorne's possible use of Goethe has but relative importance in this context. However, a possible relationship between the figure of Oberon and that of Coverdale, who may also have been vaguely influenced by Goethe, will recall the above observations near the end of the chapter. Except in these few Oberon papers, Hawthorne's further use of the pose of the frenzied youth is limited to what is hardly more than a trace of him in the detached observer, the first-person narrator of the sketches. On the other hand, the frenzied character often reappears in Hawthorne's work, in "Young Goodman Brown," for example; thus, even in Oberon there was something genuine as well as something to link *Fanshawe* and the great short stories.

Another of Hawthorne's poses in the first-person is associated with the group of picaresque incidents that were originally planned for the Story-Teller volumes. The main document is "Passages from a Relinquished Work" which includes episodes entitled "At Home," "Flight," and "Fellow Traveler," which narrates an episode that parallels an incident in *Gil Blas*. For the characterization of his picaro, Hawthorne had in mind a figure vaguely resembling Eustace Bright, later to narrate the *Tanglewood Tales*. The tone of the "Passages" suggests that Hawthorne was thinking of both a homeless Childe Harold and a naïve Gil Blas in a setting of some depth that was to be concerned with themes of the orphaned youth, the journey and the search for origins, themes which he never relinquished, as the *Ancestral Footstep*, one of the last of the novel fragments, indicates. The narrator is pleasant, reflecting, as Coverdale later does, only an exaggerated gaiety that becomes more sedate as he is later transformed into the genial narrator of "Sunday at Home" and, still later, into the serene narrator of "Night Sketches."

This pose is soon abandoned, too, except that Hawthorne remembered Gil Blas and the picaresque when he described Holgrave and perhaps remembered both Goethe and LeSage when he conceived of Coverdale. If so, Coverdale and the whole of the *Blithedale Romance* were probably conceived long before the novel was published, that is, during Hawthorne's stay at Brook Farm. The relationship to the first-person narrator of the "Passages from a Relinquished Work" and the continuing influence of Goethe would help to explain the odd appearance of a somewhat immature first-person narrator so late in Hawthorne's work, after Hawthorne had risen to the artistic height of the *Scarlet Letter*.

While Hawthorne was using these poses, one of which at least, that of the picaro, was used in the attempt to deal with the conventions of an art form that interested him, Hawthorne used two other narrators. As noted above, one was the sophisticated third-person narrator of the great short stories. The other was the relatively pleasant and natural figure of the detached observer, a first-person narrator who first appears perhaps in Oberon's friend, then as the narrator of such sketches as "Sunday at Home" and "Sights from a Steeple." One would be far more pleased to consider him rather than Coverdale to be the most genuine mask of Hawthorne. And he more than another resembles the personality of the notebooks and that of "The Old Manse," both of which presumably are genuinely Hawthorne, if any mask is. On the other hand, variants of the observer that are less pleasant appear in other sketches, sometimes with the false tone of Coverdale. Since most of the first-person narrators show traces of others, however, distinctions are relative.

Other changes in tone occur in Hawthorne's work even after he adopts the mask of the detached observer. So late even as the novel fragments, he uses, in the *Dolliver Romance*, with a somewhat false sound, a variant of this early first-person narrator and uses him in a third-person narrative. If one relates the experiments with narrative masks to an attempt that Hawthorne may have made to

find himself, one must arrive at the not unlikely conclusion that he never did find himself. Nevertheless, the pose
as observer appears to be the mask adopted for the greater
portion of Hawthorne's work during his mature period,
particularly for the allegories. During the period of the
novels, except for Coverdale, he reveals little narrative
personality, then changes to more experimentation as he
attempts to write a novel to follow the *Marble Faun*. In
view of Hawthorne's remarks about concealing personal
matters, perhaps one may conclude that giving up a narrative personality was precisely his intention.

This figure of the detached observer is also the narrator
of "Night Sketches," and by the time of its publication in
1838, the figure can be rather fully characterized, in part as
the philosophical Hawthorne. Much as Hawthorne may
have been able to conceal, he could not conceal everything. At least his themes revealed something about him.
And indeed the detached observer himself suggests a good
deal for speculation, for there is the question as to why
Hawthorne should adopt a rôle of detachment. The observer characterizes himself somewhat both in "Night
Sketches" and, later, in Coverdale's numerous remarks on
his rôle in the drama of Blithedale. The following observations on "Night Sketches" deal with the observer and with
the methods of observation developed along with the rôle.

There may have been too much attention paid of late to
Hawthorne's minor works. Yet the chance is better for
than against the possibility both that even the sketches
have depth and that with full awareness Hawthorne intended that to be the case. He so often comments on his
own methods and so carefully chooses words that one feels
more insecure in doubting the existence of a depth than in
finding a false suggestion of one. In any case, the pertinence of "Night Sketches" for the present discussion is for
other purposes than to raise another sketch to view and
offer an interpretation. There seems to be little to interpret. If the sketch was intended as an allegory of life, the
observation is too obvious to need elucidation.

"Night Sketches" is sub-titled "Beneath an Umbrella."

Eight pages of text record the observations made by the narrator as he takes a walk during a rain. He observes and moralizes, then he returns home. The tone is pleasant and genial, sometimes humorous, as in other sketches of these middle years. The mood is pensive. The narrator is vaguely characterized by this tone and mood. Two passages of outright moralization make him appear pensive in his geniality. In short, he is a dispassionate observer of life who characterizes himself as a "looker-on." Such is the pose.

Closer attention to the language reveals, however, a series of contrasts that complicate the pose. One contrast is between the humor and the seriousness. Hawthorne appears to have anticipated the use of the grotesque in the humor of the past few years. The title itself reflects the paradox, and the paradox is in Hawthorne himself. Only one of the brief episodes is described with a straightforward and unqualified tone, the very brief scene of the young "vagabond" who stands under a rainspout. The other scenes are qualified directly as presented. The stout lady is assailed by the winds. The ship's captain will narrate tales of woe. The young couple slip on the ice and fall. A contrast obviously designed to emphasize the grotesque comes just before the narrator turns homeward. Through a window he sees a family around a hearth, and he uses a few lines to describe a pleasant scene, that recalls the fireside in "John Inglefield's Thanksgiving." As in that story, the happiness is temporary and illusive. "Ye cannot damp the enjoyment of that fireside," he observes. But as a last comment on the scene, he says, "Doubt not that darker guests are sitting round the hearth, though the warm blaze hides all but blissful images" (1, 483). He notices next a brightly-lit mansion prepared for a dance. Several details fill out a pleasant scene. While the narrator watches, for example, a beautiful young woman arrives in a carriage. But immediately one recalls "Lady Eleanore's Mantle." The narrator says, "Will she ever feel the night wind and the rain? Perhaps,—perhaps! And will Death and Sorrow ever enter that proud mansion? As surely as

the dancers will be gay within its halls tonight" (1, 483).
One is not unaccustomed to this method in Hawthorne's
work of course. But the point here is to consider it as a
part of the characterization of the narrator and incidentally to point out that Hawthorne thus anticipates the
twentieth-century grotesque.

The contrast of light and dark is a favorite technique
with Hawthorne, and numerous images occur. The light
of the narrator's own fireside is contrasted with the dark
outside. During the walk, the narrator comes to the center
of town where the two rows of shops light the street.
There he observes that in the light, "The spouts gush with
fire" (1, 481). Just as he returns home, he observes a man
in the dark with a lantern. The dark is such that even
when he looks upward he can ". . . discern no sky, not
even an unfathomable void, but only a black, impenetra-
ble nothingness, as though heaven and all its lights were
blotted from the system of the universe" (1, 478–79).
Such lights as he sees serve only to ". . . show and ex-
aggerate by so faintly showing the perils and difficulties
which beset my path" (1, 479).

The many images contrasting light and dark emphasize
the setting which the narrator begins to sense immediately
on stepping into the dark as one of the "night wanderers."
Outside, he encounters basic natural phenomena, earth,
air, fire and water, all of which are confined in an elemental darkness. He hears ". . . the roaring of a stream, the
turbulent career of which is partially reddened by the
gleam of the lamp, but elsewhere brawls noisily through
the densest gloom" (1, 479). The moralization points out
that ". . . it is a cheerless scene, and cheerless are the
wanderers in it" (1, 481). Anyone concerned with the
Christianization of Hawthorne may note that the moralization, even if intended, which is doubtful, is conventional and ineffective. In view of the threats of the dark,
the moralization does little more than serve to furbish the
light images, which of course would have been better
without it. Or perhaps Hawthorne moralizes sardonically
in order to conceal the feeling of the constant encroach-

ment of the dark. Far more characteristic appears the remark, "Onward, still onward, I plunge into the night" (1, 483). The reader is never allowed to forget that the light is but enough to show the setting.

What the narrator sees in the dark in "Night Sketches" points up a technique that, as the fourth chapter indicates, Hawthorne very often uses. The narrator sees a series of broadly delineated but nameless figures who suddenly appear, act briefly and then vanish. This sketch presents a stout woman, a ship's captain, a troubled citizen, a young boy, a youthful couple, a young lady, a family, and the man with the lantern. Despite Hawthorne's moralizing and as sometimes pointed out by it, all but the boy have a qualified happiness, as noted here and there in the preceding remarks. And the boy cannot be taken as a type of Hawthorne's children. They are almost invariably either unpleasant, as those in the *Scarlet Letter* are, or they are persecuted by other children as Pearl and the gentle boy are.

There are some curious aspects to the pose that Hawthorne takes in "Night Sketches." In two respects, there are resemblances to Coverdale, who is otherwise somewhat closer to Oberon in tone. "Night Sketches" also reveals information about the pose of observer. "Luckless lovers!" the narrator says when the young couple slip on the ice and fall into the water. "Were it my nature to be other than a looker-on in life, I would attempt your rescue. Since that may not be, I vow, should you be drowned, to weave such a pathetic story of your fate as shall call forth tears enough to drown you both anew" (1, 482). This comment is reflected in Zenobia's remarks to Coverdale that he merely observes and will probably put them all in a story. Coverdale in fact rather overdoes the pose of observer.

The other point is that the narrator remarks, "Not that mine is altogether a chameleon spirit, with no hue of its own." The remark occurs just after his comment about writing the story of the young lovers and immediately after a further comment: "Onward I go, deriving a sympathetic joy or sorrow from the varied aspects of mortal affairs, even as my figure catches a gleam from the lighted windows, or is blackened by an interval of darkness" (1, 482). Coverdale takes a similar pose as sympathetic observer while also unaccountably making numerous remarks about his individuality. It is both an individuality and a sympathy that he does not particularly well maintain. And at the end of the *Blithedale Romance*, he disclaims all sympathy, presumably intent on maintaining only his individuality. Holgrave has meanwhile been portrayed as being unsympathetic except in so far as his awareness of Phoebe develops into such love as he may be able to feel. Within this framework, if there is development, the conception of Coverdale preceded that of Holgrave as well as that of Kenyon, Holgrave's spiritual twin.

Hawthorne's use of the word "chameleon" sounds odd, as if he and someone else had an awareness of significance regarding it that has made him self-conscious to the point that he nearly assumes that the reader too will recognize a context for the word. An interesting context presents itself, particularly in view of numerous other echoes of *Wilhelm Meister*. Since nothing essential in the argument of the chapter depends on the validity of the suggestion, one feels the more free in offering an explanation. Goethe uses the word in describing the actress Philina. She is said to dislike an unpleasant member of the troupe, then the passage ends, "Withal, however, she was seldom disagreeable to any one, especially to men. On the contrary, people who enjoyed her acquaintance commonly ascribed to her a fine understanding; for she was what might be called a kind of *spiritual chameleon*, or *taker-on*." The italics are in the translation, which is that of Thomas Carlyle, probably what Hawthorne would have used, and it is presumably Carlyle who adds a footnote signed by the editor. "*Anempfinderin* (feeler-by, feeler-according-to) is the new, untranslatable word poorly paraphrased so. A new German word, first used here; the like of which might be useful in all languages, for it designates a class of persons extant in all countries.—Ed." [1]

Both Wilhelm and Werther are inclined to be the spiritual chameleon, in fact. Wilhelm agrees with nearly any suggestion, suffers with many of the characters and changes opinions, loyalties and loves without much direction. Nor is either of them a very pleasant character. Wilhelm certainly could have influenced the characterization and have suggested the trait of looker-on for the detached observer of "Night Sketches." And Hawthorne may have phrased his remark in "Night Sketches" as he did because of an unconscious reaction against the accusation of being a chameleon. Coverdale was probably a highly complex yet oversimplified combination of Wilhelm Meister and a reaction against him and against influence in general. Some preconception, surely, caused Hawthorne to use the first-person narrator in the *Blithedale Romance*, when he must have known that he would be accused of dealing with real and personal events, a consideration that would have delayed the publication of the *Blithedale Romance* if it was indeed written during the Brook Farm sojourn. Yet for some reason, perhaps because Hawthorne wanted an eye-witness to comment on reformers and their ideals, or because autobiography presented itself so strongly even if the main events were not real, he uses the odd figure of Coverdale. Hawthorne must have been under the influence of the narrator of the sketches and perhaps under the influence of Goethe, both romanticized in Coverdale, the most enigmatic and not the most pleasant character among Hawthorne's generally unpleasant characters. Except perhaps for Holgrave and Kenyon, who are studied examples to the contrary, Hawthorne's young men have a tendency to be chameleonic, even the hero of the *Ancestral Footstep*. Though the characteristic is explained in somewhat more depth later, Donatello characterizes himself as responding to Miriam's various moods, and when Kenyon tries to model a bust of him he continuously changes.

"Night Sketches" cannot be said to have any great depth except what may be suggested by the language alone, but as an example of Hawthorne's pose as observer, of his narrative technique, and of the moods and nature of his perceptions of the world, it reveals a good deal. The narrator is nearly serene in the isolation of his room, yet is unsettled enough to wander out of his room and walk into the night. The rain is nearly as symbolic of quiet and nonexistence as the snow image in Robert Frost's "Stopping by Woods on a Snowy Evening." The long first paragraph is a light description of the process of creative dream laid upon the real. From this imaginative world, serene and safe, the narrator goes to escape his boredom into the dark, into another world, less safe, yet inviting, and one to which Hawthorne was continually drawn. He has a protective umbrella that serves both as an accoutrement of his mental detachment and as a protection against the "fearful auguries" in the realm of the dark. Perhaps he goes even to seek company, but the company he finds are people in the dark. Thus, the sketch is a journey into the dark and a return home. The dark is filled with shadows engaged in human action or in a somewhat grotesque and unpleasant imitation of what human action might be like in an imaginable but nonexistent daylight world. The sketch shows Hawthorne's methods of constructing stories and tales on the theme of the procession or the journey. And it shows the character of the observer, a pose that was used generally thereafter as Hawthorne came to examine human action and human life. These ideas will be elaborated in the following chapters. The point to be made here is that "Night Sketches" outlines Hawthorne's method of perceiving a dark world of animate but unidentified shadows engaged in action that is generally useless.

The pose of the detached observer was complicated then by Hawthorne's own personality, by his reading, and by his attempt to find a narrative mask. Further aspects of the matter are discussed under points of view in a following chapter, and other remarks on Coverdale are made in the chapter on the *Blithedale Romance*. The lines of investigation for this chapter are involved. The general conclusions of the main theses are that Hawthorne experimented with several poses. The problem is made complex by the necessity of putting one before another in a process of development, when the chronology of publication does not substantiate such a procedure. The influences show a tendency to romanticize and idealize the self by analogies with Childe Harold and other sensitive heroes that probably include both Werther and Wilhelm Meister. This experimentation occurred after the publication of *Fanshawe* and during the period when Hawthorne was writing, in the best short stories, his best third-person narratives. Eventually, he settled on the third-person technique of these stories. What he began to observe in his detachment suggests a reason for his pose as observer. There was so much past disappointment in his own life, such obvious unhappiness everywhere he looked, and so little room for hope that a man was helpless. All one could do was adopt a mask of indifference, then observe and report. The mask of indifference was thus probably a defense against intimacy and disappointment.

HAWTHORNE IS ENIGMATIC in all respects, both in his life and in his work. Despite a curiosity, one is inclined to leave him with whatever quite personal secrets he may have had, as he tended ultimately to do with his characters. Yet his tendency to leave them their secrets derived in part from the same source as the critic's tendency— ignorance and inability to conclude. Meanwhile, like the critic, Hawthorne speculates to a point that nearly arrives at the violation of individuality that he seems to disapprove of, particularly of the female characters in his work. Coverdale's examination of Zenobia is an example. As a novelist, Hawthorne of course has the right to study violation as an aspect of the study of human action, which was the main interest of the detached observer. Behind this mask nevertheless is the character of the author, some of whose personal interests appear to come into view when the themes are studied.

The comments in the preceding chapter on *Fanshawe* and *Septimius Felton* indicated that Hawthorne created a plot designed to leave the bohemian, the artist, or the more sensitive of two youths free of the love entanglement. A good reason for suggesting that the *Blithedale Romance* was conceived and perhaps written long before it was published is that Coverdale follows the pattern set by Fanshawe. If one does not assume that the variants of this theme belong to Hawthorne's early period, one must recognize that the theme occupied him throughout his life, at the time of publication of *Fanshawe* in 1828, at the time of publication of the *Blithedale Romance* in 1852, and during the later years of his life when presumably one of his concerns was with *Septimius Felton*. This may be true. There is no thesis to propound that requires a change in the usual chronology. The only point is to resolve the questions as well as possible. Success or failure in resolving the question of chronology does not affect the study of the themes but only of their development, while the study of development may somewhat elucidate the problem of chronology. If *Septimius Felton* belongs to the period of the other novel fragments, it goes even further than the *Blithedale Romance* in breaking lines of development, for both the *House of the Seven Gables* and the *Marble Faun* have presented resolved love situations. A trace of the tendency to withdraw may remain in the *Marble Faun* in Kenyon's refusal to listen to Miriam's confession, but that can be explained, as it is in a later chapter, on the theory of indifference. Donatello is withdrawn from Miriam, and the supposed heir of the *Ancestral Footstep* shows no particular concern for the young woman. But Donatello and Miriam do apparently have a love affair before Donatello gives himself up, and the intention in the *Ancestral Footstep* may have been to have the disappointed heir return to America with a bride. Yet, the following chapters leave both *Septimius Felton* and the *Blithedale Romance* in their usual places.

Many of the suggestions in the next few pages anticipate ideas that are discussed in more detail in the other essays. Unfortunately, the frequent indication of such may be distracting. In addition, other lines of investigation are inconclusive because one has no assurance about resolutions. There are, however, a good many interesting details behind Hawthorne's masks, and noting them is of some value even if one does not know how to use them for seeing behind the mask.

Many other factors must be considered in the discussion of Hawthorne's treatment of the theme of love and marriage that was introduced in the preceding chapter. Among these are incidents dealing with young lovers, those dealing with violations and those dealing with miscellaneous aspects of the theme of love. The question of sex occupies Hawthorne throughout his writing career, though it is less intrusive after publication of the *Marble Faun*. *Fanshawe* presents the Gothic theme of the attempted rape. Ellen's appearance at the hotel hints briefly of a secret affair. If "Alice Doane's Appeal" is one of Hawthorne's earliest stories, he was interested very early in incest. "The Hollow of the Three Hills" presents a woman who has abandoned her family ties, much as John Inglefield's daughter does. Many of the other works are mentioned below under categories dealing with other aspects of the themes.

Among the categories is that of tales of estrangement and unhappiness. Roger Malvin's feelings of guilt cause him to be estranged from Dorcas, in a situation that somewhat resembles that of "Young Goodman Brown" after Brown's experience in the forest. "The Canterbury Pilgrims" presents a couple who have lost their regard for one another. Wakefield leaves his wife for twenty years. The happy pair in "The Maypole of Merrymount" are chastened by church and state, in a situation that anticipates that of Donatello and Miriam. Mr. Hooper, the minister, conceals his face from his fiancée as well as his parishioners. "The Wedding Knell" ends with a sardonic commentary on marriage. "The Prophetic Pictures" deals with the story of a man who possesses a compulsion to kill presumably the woman he will love. Richard Digby, the man of adamant, deserts his fiancée and everyone else. "Mrs. Bullfrog" is, despite its apparent lack of seriousness, a sardonic commentary on the ideal woman. "Edward Fane's Rosebud" is a story of unrequited love. Lady Eleanore scorns her suitor. "The Lily's Quest" is a story of unhappy love. Beatrice and Giovanni, in "Rappaccini's Daughter," literally poison each other by being what they are. Obviously, the love entanglements in Hawthorne's work suggest but little of the new Adam and Eve. Rather, they repeat what is likely to have occurred to the first Adam and Eve after the expulsion from Eden.

After the withdrawal of *Fanshawe*, Hawthorne continues to eliminate the more sensitive of the young men from the love triangle. The *Blithedale Romance* and others were mentioned above. The obvious example, however, is "The Artist of the Beautiful." Owen Warland resembles Fanshawe and Septimius in having concerns that prevent him from exerting himself with regard to the girl whom he is presumed to love. And in this story, the pleasant Walcott has become the boorish Robert Danforth. "The Artist of the Beautiful" suggests that the sensitive youth as artist withdraws from all intimacies, not that of the marriage relationship alone. This may be the suggestion made by all the other works that deal with the theme.

The related theme of violation naturally arises here for some preliminary remarks. Violation, as Hawthorne uses the term, apparently means the traduction of the individuality of another, with overtones of physical seduction. Possibly some would feel that the theme was first introduced in *Fanshawe* in the villain's attempt to rape Ellen. Another possible source is "Young Goodman Brown," which, as it turned out, was something of a preliminary study for the *Scarlet Letter*. In both, the man and woman apparently violated each other, in that each is known to the other under conditions that lead to severe judgments. In "Young Goodman Brown" the experience of mutual violation must be confined to the forest episode, since no indication is given that Faith shares Brown's disillusionment. In these examples, the violation appears to be mutual. Usually, however, the cases of violation are explicitly one-sided. Thus, perhaps the first actual use of the theme is in "Sylph Etherege," a story of a man's cruelly deceiving a young woman for little apparent reason. Violation in this story would hardly be noticed, however, if Hawthorne had not later emphasized the concept.

Hawthorne's emphasis on the theme appears heaviest in "The Birthmark" of 1843. In this story, the theme is associated with the concept of the ideal woman, and the action ends in the sensitive youth's depriving himself of the young woman, as Fanshawe does. "Ethan Brand," which also uses the theme of violation, was apparently intended to suggest that violation of the individuality of another was the unpardonable sin, unpardonable probably in Hawthorne's fancy, without any theological implications at all. The novels deal with the theme of violation too. Zenobia suffers not from Coverdale alone, but from all the males in the *Blithedale Romance*, as will be discussed in more detail in a later essay. Priscilla suffers from both Westervelt and Hollingsworth. The narrative hints that Miriam was violated somehow by the man in disguise. And the *House of the Seven Gables* uses the theme to suggest a reason for the enervation of the curse. Hawthorne rather explicitly puts Holgrave and Phoebe in a situation that could lead to physical seduction and points out that Holgrave respects Phoebe's innocence. He restrains himself from committing the act of either physical seduction or violation of individuality, one or both of which acts Matthew Maule presumably committed against Alice Pyncheon, thus extending the term of the curse.

The remarkable aspect of the theme of violation in Hawthorne's work is that in the examples cited, a man always violates the individuality of a woman. This tendency is even more interesting in view of the fact that Hawthorne also allows his sensitive youths to withdraw from the sexual conflicts. Yet another of Hawthorne's conventions, to be discussed in more detail later, is that Hawthorne creates a group of women who make men ordinary. Ellen, Phoebe, and Hilda draw their husbands out of the conflicts of the world, in situations paralleling the tendency of the more sensitive youths to die, retire, or simply withdraw. Stories of the cruelty of women are very rare, though stories of enigmatic women abound. Hawthorne was fascinated indeed by the secrets of the women he created, even Hepzibah. All four of the novels have strong female characters, and all but the *House of the Seven Gables* deal integrally with the deepest secrets of these women. Hepzibah's turban, a symbol of her dreams of the exotic, suggests that Hawthorne considered providing a shadowy past for her, too, particularly in view of his presenting her as devoted to her Sybarite brother. "Rappaccini's Daughter," in this context, is a preliminary study on the theme of the enigmatic women, and it may be the exoticism of Beatrice herself that accounts for the single exotic setting in Hawthorne's work.

The source that suggests itself as the origin of Hawthorne's interest in the theme of violation, even if it does not contain precisely the first example, is "Young Goodman Brown." Does the story record an experience that really occurred to Hawthorne? At the high-point of the initiation ceremony, Goodman Brown shouts, " 'Faith! Faith! . . . look up to heaven, and resist the wicked one' " (II, 105). To judge from Goodman Brown's later actions, Faith did not respond, and Brown himself was left in utter disillusionment. The experience was intense enough to change the whole course of his life, however. If the story derived from an autobiographical experience, it could have led both to Hawthorne's portrayal of violations of women and to his compensating disapproval of such acts. Here, too, the discussion is not greatly affected by the speculation. At some point after the publication of "Young Goodman Brown," Hawthorne quite explicitly portrayed scenes of violation. The possible relationship between the portrayals and autobiography need not be forced beyond speculation. The question remains whether there is a relationship between the sensitive youth's willingness to sacrifice the young woman and the later interest in stories of masculine cruelty, both within a framework of an overt concern with sex, and a still later curiosity about exotic and secretive women. As suggested later, it may be that Hawthorne's interest in the theme of violation derives from Milton. Since the influence of Milton's *Paradise Lost*, or Hawthorne's simple awareness of it, seems particularly clear in "Young Goodman Brown," there is a touch of support for the suggestion that "Young Goodman Brown" is related to the development of the interest in violation. Too, much of Hawthorne's work deals with the intense experience that both enlightens and destroys, as is the case with Brown. Generally, before and after publication of "Young Goodman Brown," the narrator reveals a sympathy for the women, as in Ellen's case, except in the treatment of Zenobia. Perhaps Brown's experience makes women enigmatic by removing them from the ideal world and making them human.

On the other hand, *Paradise Lost* shows the man and woman violating each other in their mutual feelings of lust and in their knowledge of each other's humanity. That too apparently happens in the initiation ceremony with Faith, as Brown perceives the experience under the devil's injunction to them both to view each other. The story ignores some of these details in emphasizing Brown's experience alone. But it was Brown's experience, and one of the things he learned was about the humanity of women. Since the idea explicit in both *Paradise Lost* and "Young Goodman Brown" is that the violation is mutual, one might be prepared for what occurs in Hawthorne's work, which is treatments of violation that are *not* those of men against women. Though the existence of other kinds of violation does not explain the several examples of the tendency to write scenes of the violation of women, apparently Hawthorne gradually arrived at the very broad definition of the term.

Violation came to mean any attempt to manipulate others. With this in mind, one recalls other examples. In the *Blithedale Romance* Hollingsworth unsuccessfully tries to dominate Coverdale. One of the most overt of violations is Chillingworth's investigation of Dimmesdale. Perhaps the Judge violates both Hepzibah and Clifford. Other suggestions will be made from time to time below. Hawthorne seems to have arrived eventually at the idea that human relationships were usually violations or attempted violations. And examples of those situations are what he chose to portray, thus concentrating on a group of fairly unpleasant characters. Whatever influence his own peculiarities had on his perceptions, Hawthorne must hardly have had a pleasant acquaintance.

A minor point causes an interesting complication in the discussion. Though unhappy loves abound in his work, Hawthorne sometimes presents the figures of young lovers, such as those in "Night Sketches" and in "The Seven Vagabonds." These are charming, fresh couples who appear for a moment then vanish, usually. It is of the young couple in "Night Sketches" that he promises to write a pathetic story in case something happens to them. Yet one points out their occurrence merely in order to indicate that they are not overlooked, for they are rare, charming as they may be. Not all are charming. An over-sentimentalized couple appear in "The Great Carbuncle," and "The Canterbury Pilgrims" shows a youthful pair advised by a disillusioned older couple. The couple depart from the meeting with only a chastened enthusiasm, while they are determined apparently to take their chance in the world. More often, however, the young lovers resemble those of "The Lily's Quest," and the point is made poignant in the case of Donatello and Miriam. They, too, are presented somewhat as young lovers when the story opens and at the end. But they love under the realization that their happiness must soon end in Donatello's imprisonment. And their separation during the greater part of the story as well as at the end of it is more characteristic of Hawthorne's work than their brief union is. Only "The Wives of the Dead" presents what appears to be a successful ending to a love story. In so far as Kenyon and Hilda or Holgrave and Phoebe may represent the young couples, they are discussed below in the material on the novels in which they appear.

Yet another aspect of Hawthorne's mask must be noted. In the novel fragments, he makes a change in narrative methods. In *Fanshawe* the intimacy is with Ellen. In the *Scarlet Letter*, it is with Hester, though in both cases hesitant, for Hawthorne never shows much intimacy with any of his characters. Perhaps he disapproved of most of them. But in the novel fragments of the *Ancestral Foot-*

step, he creates in Redclyffe a relatively pleasant character who seems quite genuine and quite autobiographical. Thus, Hawthorne resolved the question of his own mask. Yet, both retaining the enigma and complicating it, he gave up the figure of Redclyffe, leaving in fact the question of whether he ever found himself.

Why does Hawthorne so frequently use the theme of the unlucky lovers or that of the traduced individuality of the woman? Speculations of this kind always suggest the worst, particularly in view of hints of one sort or another now and then about what Hawthorne may have had to conceal. And there seems to be little doubt that both he and the family concealed a great deal. But Hawthorne was much too complex a man to be labeled with any particular tag. And indeed despite various suggestions that might be made, the indication is of an awareness of extreme sensitivity and a fear of intimacy not easily overcome. These, indeed, are troubles enough, and it may be that even if one had more words and another language he would know no more.

Whatever else may be true, Hawthorne must have had an experience or a series of experiences that led him to concentrate on women, somewhat to sympathize with them, but also to reveal some degree of interest in showing them as being unhappy. He does not usually show them married or as mothers. Pearl and a few others are exceptions, but Pearl herself is an indication that nothing particularly good comes in the progeny. The portrayal of unhappy marriages or unhappy lovers fits with Hawthorne's general view as discussed throughout the following pages. No one is particularly happy, not merely the women. By the time of the allegories, Hawthorne was the seer, the philosophical observer, and unhappiness is what he saw. The pose had become genuine, and for some time to come the themes discussed above nearly vanished from Hawthorne's work. It was as if he saw their meaning and feared the revelations about himself. After a brief spell of what may have been happiness in his marriage, he returned to his old themes in writing the novels. At that point, he reveals a pessimism that is serene on the surface. Something is lost, however, with the lost freshness of his doubts. He appears to have stopped doubting, on the conviction that there was no doubt.

AS HAWTHORNE BEGINS to codify his thought and show development in his work, he deals first with humanity in the abstract. The allegories of the Manse period, for example, result not from a dearth of material but from the musing of a philosophic story-teller. The musing is much concerned with formidable questions, because Hawthorne is trying to see things whole that will not fit. Man is outlined against life, and the two—man and life—are seen to be for the most part antagonistic, one having to put up with the other. Life exists in a twilit world into which shadowy figures emerge from the dark, act for a moment, then disappear. At the beginning of "The Procession of Life," where all human kind is reorganized on such principles as intelligence and love, Hawthorne says, "Life figures itself to me as a festal or funereal procession. All of us have our places, and are to move onward under the direction of the Chief Marshal" (II, 235), who is Death. An allegory naturally is not concerned with individuals, but the philosophy and technique are not confined to the allegories. In the allegories and some of the earlier tales, perhaps under the influence of the Greek dramatists, Hawthorne creates figures who act under forces and passions that are responsible for their actions. In the novels, action is distorted by individuality and interrelationships.

Hawthorne frequently allegorizes life by setting up an enclosure or a stage. Perhaps, because he sees the world in terms of disturbing ambiguities and contraries, he always imagines some kind of bond, often a mere generalization, that seems to him to correlate, while emphasizing, diversity. Figures then move about, briefly displaying whatever characteristics show the relationship that gives them momentary existence. The bond may consist of a quest for the great carbuncle, for the living image of the great stone face or for another symbol of the ideal. It may be provided by a general wish to escape the world, as is the case with the Canterbury pilgrims. Or the bond may be nothing more than the museum in which all the oddities of a virtuoso are collected. Often, the only bond is provided by the narrator of a sketch, who moves around and describes what he sees, as in "Sights from a Steeple."

The bond is usually integral with the plot, providing unity, as in "David Swan." More often the bond is provided by the goal toward which the procession moves. Wandering quests are made in "The Man of Adamant," in "My Kinsman, Major Molyneux," and in numerous other stories. Almost every tale and sketch contains some kind of procession, however loosely formed. Formal ones occur in "The Gray Champion" and "Howe's Masquerade." There are a few bridal processions, one in "The Wedding Knell" and one in "The Maypole of Merrymount," neither of them "festal." The ghosts parade and shift about in "Alice Doane's Appeal," as they do in "The Old Woman's Tale" and at Judge Pyncheon's death. Several chapters of the *Marble Faun* deal with the procession of the artists in the moonlight through Rome. Others deal with the journey of Kenyon, Donatello, and Miriam back to Rome from Monte Beni, a pilgrimage for all of them. Processions of numerous pilgrims and of the carnival figures also appear in the *Marble Faun*, with numerous catalogues of sights and sculptures. In *Septimius Felton* there are two martial parades, and others appear in "Earth's Holocaust" and "Sights from a Steeple"; a retreat is talked of in "Roger Malvin's Burial" and a loose battle formation appears in "The Maypole of Merrymount."

Catalogues occur in "Time's Portraiture" and in "Brown's Folly," where a parade of clothing reveals itself in the closet. Collections of one kind or another occur in "A Bell's Biography," in "Old News," where there is a list of ills and disturbances, and in "Young Goodman Brown," where there is a catalogue of sins. There is a list of Hepzibah's wares in the *House of the Seven Gables*, and a list is given of the books in Aylmer's library.

"The Intelligence Office," itself an allegory of life, shows both the procession and the collection. Among those who visit the Office are "a ruddy Irish girl . . . a single gentleman . . . Peter Schlemihl . . . or an author . . ." (II, 364). Among the collected items are "wedding rings . . . ivory tablets . . . withered flowers . . . locks of hair . . . gold pencil cases . . ." (II, 369). Hawthorne says at the end of another list of items deposited in the Office that "Most of them, doubtless, had a history and a meaning, if there were time to search it out and room to tell it" (II, 369–70). Such was often the point of the many collections, perhaps, and when Hawthorne found that he could not always search out the meaning by writing a story like "The Antique Ring," he simply wrote a sketch like "A Virtuoso's Collection," in which he listed his curiosities and possible themes.

In the *American Notebooks* Hawthorne says he would like "To sit down in a solitary place (or a busy and bustling one, if you please) and await such little events as may happen, or observe such noticeable points as the eyes fall upon around you" (102). And what he thus observed he categorized. Persons and objects were placed by means of insight, knowledge, or whimsy. Thus, the cataloguing is the establishment of things that are. An ego observes and says, this is. Then, some, often vague, principle of organization is devised to show interrelationships, as if to provide secret knowledge but perhaps also in order to provide assurance for Hawthorne himself.

A good illustration of the setting onto which Hawthorne precipitates his figures is "An Old Woman's Tale." Anticipating James in, for example, *What Maisie Knew*, the story moves through the various levels of narrative point of view to concentrate on the dream legend, then on specific figures in the crowd, suggesting that passions existed which might now be used for story telling. The ghosts appear, act their former parts for a moment, then vanish.

Life plunges into the scene in "Old Ticonderoga." Out of the forest quiet, "A light paddle dips into the lake, a birch canoe glides round the point, and an Indian chief has passed . . ." (III, 594). A moment later, "a white flag caught the breeze, over a castle in the wilderness, with frowning ramparts and a hundred cannon. There stood a French chevalier . . ." (III, 595). Thus are they introduced.

In "The Canterbury Pilgrims" a long paragraph describes the setting in the moonlight by the spring. Then, "While the moon was hanging almost perpendicularly over this spot, two figures appeared on the summit of the hill, and came with noiseless footsteps down towards the spring" (III, 518), their entry as abrupt as the Indian chief's. The clause, "Suddenly, there was seen the figure of an ancient man . . ." (I, 26), introduces the Mosaic figure of the gray champion. In "A Select Party," the Man of Fancy "now discerned another guest, who stood so quietly in the shadow of one of the pillars that he might easily have been overlooked" (II, 73), like Old Moodie. Young Goodman Brown is particularly aware of the sudden appearance in the twilight of a figure who turns out to be the devil (II, 90). In "Sunday at Home," when the church bell rings, "the sidewalks of the street, both up and down along, are immediately thronged with two long lines of people . . ." (I, 35). In "Night Sketches," from a pool of water, a young man and woman "emerge like a water nymph and a river deity . . ." (I, 482). In "Howe's Masquerade," the crowd watches a procession coming out of the darkness at the head of the stairway, "although so dusky was the region whence it emerged, some of the spectators fancied that they had seen this human shape suddenly moulding itself amid the gloom" (I, 287). In "The Threefold Destiny," at twilight, "a tall, dark figure, over which long and remote travel had thrown an outlandish aspect, was entering a village . . ." (I, 527).

The *Blithedale Romance* has a good many examples of the sudden appearance of a character. "Our greetings were hardly concluded, when the door opened, and Zenobia . . . entered . . ." (III, 13). "Soon, with a tremendous stamping in the entry, appeared Silas Foster . . ." (III, 18). The use of footsteps as preparation suggests precipitance too, though the noise with which Silas enters may be intended to show the difference between his openness and the secrecy of all the others. Precipitance is particularly associated with Old Moodie. When Coverdale waits for him in the tavern, he says, ". . . all at once, I recognized his hand and arm, protruding from behind a screen . . ." (III, 178); he habitually "glided about like a spirit, assuming visibility close to your elbow . . ." (III, 179).

Hawthorne summarizes the process himself in "The Haunted Mind," speaking of the phantoms of a dream, "In both [the dream and human life] you emerge from mystery, pass through a vicissitude that you can but imperfectly control, and are borne onward to another mystery" (I, 348). Indeed, figures vanish as suddenly as they come. Near the end of "Old Ticonderoga," as the veteran lights his pipe, "they all vanish in a puff of smoke from the chimney" (III, 596), to return only when some dreamer summons them (III, 597). Feathertop vanishes through the door into the Deacon's house, as he had, not long before, vanished from Mother Rigby's sight by turning a corner. How lightly substanced the figures are is particularly clear from a comment in "Old News." "Along the ghostly street . . . , there are ghostly people too. . . . Make way; for the whole spectral show will vanish, if your earthly garments brush against their robes" (III, 553). Coverdale says of Priscilla, "I almost imagined her a shadow, fading gradually into the dimness of the wood" (III, 125), like the white old maid and old Esther Dudley. And though the process is a lingering one, surely the same is true of more outstanding characters in

Hawthorne. For Hester vanishes gradually into much the same kind of greyness, in a brief scene at the end. Kenyon and Holgrave are to be absorbed by society, another kind of vanishing.

A variant of Hawthorne's method, coming somewhere between the outright submergence of the character and the frequent use of such mechanical analogies as the puppet show or the magic box, is exemplified by a brief descriptive passage in the *Blithedale Romance*. Coverdale says, ". . . I saw a concourse of strange figures beneath the overshadowing branches; they appeared, and vanished, and came again . . ." (III, 209). Later, as Coverdale observes the apartment houses the "respectable mistress of the boarding-house made a momentary transit across the kitchen-window, and appeared no more" (III, 151). In "Wives of the Dead" Mary watches the departure of the man who brought news, "with a doubt of waking reality, that seemed stronger or weaker as he alternately entered the shade of the houses, or emerged into the broad streaks of moonlight" (III, 605). Their appearances are momentary and transient.

Hawthorne had proposed in the *American Notebooks*, "To allegorize life with a masquerade, and represent mankind generally as masquers. Here and there, a natural face may appear" (99). This is the method and the philosophy of his work. The long carnival scene of the *Marble Faun* does precisely this. A striking passage from "Night Scene," also recorded in the notebooks, and perhaps influenced by a recollection of James Fenimore Cooper's *The Deerslayer*, summarizes the method. "Some wild Irishmen were replenishing our stock of wood, and had kindled a great fire on the bank to illuminate their labors. . . . [T]he Irishmen were continually emerging from the dense gloom, passing through the lurid glow, and vanishing into the gloom on the other side. Sometimes a whole figure would be made visible . . . ; others were but half-seen, like imperfect creatures; many flitted, shadow-like, along the skirts of darkness . . . ; and often, a face alone was reddened by the fire, and stared strangely distinct, with no traces of a body. In short, these wild Irish, distorted and exaggerated by the blaze, now lost in deep shadow, now bursting into sudden splendor, and now struggling between light and darkness . . . [resembled] devils condemned to keep alive the flames of their own torments" xii, 21–22). Some version of this scene appears in "The Celestial Railroad," (ii, 221–22), "Young Goodman Brown," (ii, 100), and "The Vision of the Fountain" (i, 243).

Though Hawthorne often uses natural settings in his early stories, he usually shows a background onto which he precipitates characters; and nature recedes, even if the characters themselves are but shadows moving through its tall forests, in and out of its light and shadow, themselves like shades, soon moving on to leave the face of nature impassive and unchanged. Perhaps nature and human existence really take little thought of each other; the characters are puppets, shadows in the light, silhouettes put onto a screen by magic. Nature is the magic screen at times, but rather by chance; not because natural scenery is needed but because the author is interested in that too.

Figures appear and disappear, then; and while they are alive, they are isolated and detached from nature and from compassion like Goodman Brown. Perhaps the most outstanding scene in "The Intelligence Office," a sketch that in general summarizes Hawthorne's whole method, presents an ill-dressed man who wears "the characteristic expression of a man out of his right place." Replying to the Intelligence Officer's question, he says, " 'I want . . . a place!' " not, Hawthorne says, "in a physical or intellectual sense, but with an urgent moral necessity that is the hardest of all things to satisfy, since it knows not its own object." Then the man repeats his wish, more frenzied. " 'I want my place! my own place! my true place in the world! my proper sphere! my thing to do, which nature intended me to perform when she fashioned me thus awry, and which I have vainly sought all my lifetime!' " (ii, 364–65). The language that the man uses, though one of despair, considerably understates the urgency of the search as it is presented in the greater part of Hawthorne's work. The number of displaced is sufficient that Hawthorne collects them separately in "The Procession of Life," where he indicates that the group is composed of the many who never found themselves or who did so too late.

The man is to some extent representative of most of Hawthorne's characters. Fanshawe, who has only a last name, has no antecedents. Holgrave is an orphan, like both the ambitious guest and Goodman Brown. Miriam and Zenobia are suspected of having pasts, never fully revealed, and members of such families as they have only plague them. Donatello comes from a mythical past. It is a part of Robin's story and David Swan's that they are isolated from their families, and they remain alone. The gentle boy thinks himself orphaned, which for the most part is true, and he remains a stranger to his foster parents. The American claimant of the romance fragments is from the almshouse, and, in the resolutions that Hawthorne left, remains unknown to himself. Septimius is an orphan with a vaguely supernatural background. Almost none of the numerous marriages that are mentioned in Hawthorne's work ends happily. Lovers are abandoned and parents are left at home. A birth rarely occurs. Children are few, and most of them are unhappy. Domestic manners, the home itself, despite whatever interest Hawthorne may have had in hearth and heart, are somewhere behind or before the character. Each could write the journal of a solitary man, and some would have to write notes from the underground. And Hawthorne does not urge them to go home or to be happy. He assumes that they will not be.

Figures are not only isolated; they are detached and indifferent. Coverdale, though he at first talks a good deal about sympathy, disclaims an interest in humanity. Holgrave only watches events in the *House of the Seven Gables*, and Kenyon rejects Miriam's confidence. Everyone is isolated except the pleasant but insignificant young lovers, and once they join they live anonymously. Ellen

Langton had an "almost imperceptible, but powerful influence, [that] drew her husband away from the passions and pursuits that would have interfered with domestic felicity; and he never regretted the worldly distinction of which she thus deprived him" (III, 460). Hawthorne's reasonable young men, Holgrave and Kenyon, who fall into line behind Walcott, choose the eternal feminine. The other, more individualistic and more frenzied group, who fall into line behind Fanshawe, move rapidly toward death, a surer way to peace. Perhaps, Hawthorne regrets the isolation, but except for ineffectual moralizing in such tales as "Wakefield," he does not urge an end to the isolation, not, at least, by sharing, by love, or even by sympathy. Hawthorne's characters would appear quite selfish if they were not so unhappy. Their wandering actions are only errant, hopeless searches for the end. Hawthorne's "good" characters are not pleasant. Toward the "bad" ones, like Hester, Zenobia, and Miriam, he is for the most past indifferent.

Place for the outcasts can be found only in death. In the *House of the Seven Gables*, just before Clifford tries to leap from the window, the narrator says that from a distance a procession "melts all the petty personalities" composing it "into one broad mass of existence,—one great life, one collected body of mankind . . ." (III, 199). If an "impressible person . . . [felt the] mighty river of life, massive in its tide, and black with mystery, and, out of its depths, calling to the kindred depth within him . . . he would hardly be restrained from plunging into the surging stream of human sympathies" (III, 199–200). Clifford's attempt to lose his individuality in the whole, an action that results from an innate desire, is an attempt at suicide. And the Intelligence Office, with its depository of desires and potential satisfaction, is located on the border of the realm of the pleasure principle, where the death wish can be granted by an omnipotent figure.

The many quests that appear in Hawthorne's work are journeys without goals. Much happens, but no goal is reached, in part because none exists, in part because one forgets what his goal is, and in part because there is no way of reaching it. In addition, there is probably no use. Redclyffe (a generic name for the hero of the novel fragments), for example, searches vaguely and hesitantly, and when about convinced of being the heir, discovers that he is not. All his actions are based on a false assumption. Left not knowing who he is, he may start over, perhaps as the new Adam. But for Hawthorne the potential beginning as the new Adam and Eve is not only a wish for the return of innocence, it is also a sign of being immensely tired in a world that needs an "age-long" nap. All other beginnings were failures.

Hawthorne's work as a whole is an elaboration of the useless desires listed in the Book of Wishes kept in the Intelligence Office; or excerpts from the darker pages of the great folio. Hawthorne shows the forces and the desires that motivate action. He materializes archetypes and presents an abstract of life, describing what he sees. Always nearby is the man whom none can help, the early visitor to the Intelligence Office who wants to know who he is and where his place is, strongly implying that he wishes to be at peace. Hawthorne appears to offer a reply to the main question. Ethan Brand commits suicide. Though the circumstances may appear less serious, Feathertop, on realizing himself, does the same. Dimmesdale's life seems to be an enactment of the death wish. The man of adamant chooses a cave, and Donatello chooses a cell.

HAWTHORNE EXPERIMENTS a good deal with points of view. To some extent, he, like Lawrence Sterne and Jane Austen, anticipates the vague stream-of-consciousness movement of the twentieth century. Sterne's random style is as one likes it, charming, boring, annoying. Austen uses *style indirect libre* with a pleasant and natural ease. Hawthorne usually reveals tension. Though he seems unaware of the technique of *style indirect libre* or of inner monologue, his characters often seem to urge him to devise some method that will give them the freedom to think. The methods that he devises are the more interesting because he generally uses types or representative figures, which he keeps under strict control. Paradoxically, these unindividualized and "masked" types are aware of one another. Techniques often appear to be designed to provide immediacy. Despite the degree of truth in T. S. Eliot's claim that Hawthorne's characters are the first before those of James to be aware of one another, Hawthorne seems interested in keeping his characters mentally isolated both from one another and from the reader. He often enough allows characters to interact, particularly in the novels, where the enigma of being is analyzed. But the author remains as ignorant of information as the other characters do. Neither the author nor anyone else ever knows Miriam or Hester, for example. Control is implicit in this method of course. And the method is realistic; only what is known within the framework of the action is revealed. There is a suggestion that more intimacy would somehow violate individuality. Yet, also, the character never really has the chance to reveal himself, though he often seems to wish to do so. Thus, in narrative technique as well as in characterization, Hawthorne prevents his characters from being known.

A possible reason for Hawthorne's control was that he simply wished to avoid intimacies with his characters in order to avoid revealing himself by projection. Probably more important, however, he wished to create figures in the tradition of classical drama. The mask that hid individuality in Greek drama is replaced by a control that prevents revelation of idiosyncrasies. By this means, the actors in Hawthorne's dramas are types and figures that show the effects of forces beyond their control. Hawthorne's avoidance of characterization may result from this concern with displaying the force that influences action, particularly since the motives for human action were one of his main interests.

The attempt to control is not always successful, and the failure sometimes adds to one's appreciation of Hawthorne's work. Hepzibah got out of hand, probably, and enhanced the effect of the *House of the Seven Gables*. The novel fragments apparently were never controlled, yet the method used in some fragments, where if anywhere Hawthorne employed *style indirect libre*, might have led to the writing of a greater novel than any of those Hawthorne completed. Aware as the Puritans may have been of a kind of classical fatalism in which the supernatural often intervened in the affairs of men, there is something incongruous in Hawthorne's attempt to recreate the milieu and use "masked" figures. Yet, almost in spite of himself, it seems, Hawthorne's development is toward the creation of self-awareness in his characters. The development moves from the isolated scene to the highly conscious narration of the *Ancestral Footstep*.

In isolated scenes, a good many characters have moments of awareness, which are presented to the reader with various degrees of immediacy. Perhaps, indeed, the account of these epiphanies is the central intent of the better tales: "Young Goodman Brown," "Roger Malvin's Burial," "My Kinsman, Major Molyneux." The point is emphasized in "The Man of Adamant," wherein conditions are most intense and wherein the character utterly rejects the potential for a moment of self-awareness, or in "David Swan," wherein the intent is to show the potential of the unknown.

The reader cannot always share the intensity of the experience because Hawthorne does not allow the character to be quite alive. Owen Warland's moment has occurred when he delivers the butterfly, and what occurs in the last scene is anti-climactic. Chillingworth has a moment of awareness in which he realizes that he is "a fiend," but Hawthorne only describes the occurrence. He shows no change and allows no intimacy. Donatello has an intensely shattering experience when he throws the monk from the wall, but Hawthorne does little more to make the experience dramatic than to show the long penance. The change in Donatello is but described, in attenuated tones.

Clifford's monologue on the train successfully reveals thought without use of inner monologue. Intoxicated by heightened emotions, Clifford talks a great deal, relieving his mind of tensions and prejudices incurred during the many years of harsh treatment. The scene is the greater for the fact that Clifford is but for a short time so mentally active, expressing ideas that he probably does in fact not hold, if one judges by his docility afterwards.

And much the same technique is used with Dimmesdale as he returns from the meeting with Hester. Both characters reveal Hawthorne's intuitive awareness of the psychologically true. A part of his greatness derives from the subtle use of touches that one but gradually comes to appreciate. The scene is expressionistic, anticipating the later, primarily German, literary movement. Both Dimmesdale and Clifford show the stream of the unconscious, the one in a detached and descriptive third-person narration, the other by an uncontrolled babbling. Yet, the scene presenting Dimmesdale's return from the forest is a thorough failure. Hawthorne controls Dimmesdale, but not himself. His technique involves the somewhat childish irony that chides Judge Pyncheon. Psychologically, Dimmesdale's actions seem entirely true, but the handling is self-conscious, moralistic, and unpleasantly ironic.

Whatever his intention, Hawthorne attempts an experiment in technique that is far separate from inner monologue but that seems nevertheless designed to achieve intimacy. This is the technique of the traditional frame story. Hawthorne made use of the method in the children's books. But he appears to want to achieve something more than a frame or an enclosed tale. The use of the "Custom-House" sketch as a preface to the *Scarlet Letter* is the result of this wish. But the method is first tried in "Alice Doane's Appeal." Here, Hawthorne tries to do what he proposed for the Story Teller volume, to give a "sketch of the circumstances in which the story was told," presenting "characteristic figures, amid the lake and mountain scenery, the villages and fertile fields, of our native land" (II, 461). In the children's books he settles for the mere frame, but in "Alice Doane's Appeal," by putting his listeners on Gallows Hill and in a setting elaborate with eerie associations, he tries to make the drama of the tale far more real to them. He tries to integrate the story with the experience of it, and he notes that the audience of girls are in fact affected by hearing the tale in these associative surroundings. As a narrative technique of course it fails. But Hawthorne was probably trying to put a narrative on the stage. He tries again in the *House of the Seven Gables*, where he records a good deal more success than the reader feels. Holgrave's story of Alice, intended also as exposition, is accompanied by such movements as to mesmerize Phoebe and cause her to fall asleep. Here, at least according to Hawthorne, the dramatic situation of the narrative impinges on real life and has an intense effect. A similar, rather less obvious attempt at dramatic immediacy occurs in the *Blithedale*

Romance, in Zenobia's story of the veil, which ends with her throwing the cloth over Priscilla. The story of the Spectre of the Catacombs probably derives from a similar attempt, and so may the account of Donatello's examination of Miriam's portfolio.

Goethe's *Wilhelm Meister's Apprenticeship* may have suggested this technique to Hawthorne. In Book VII, when Theresa meets Wilhelm for the purpose of relating the account of her past, she appears in a huntsman's costume and explains, " '. . . I will recall those days, by every method, to my fancy. Come along! Even the place, where we have rested so often from our hunts and promenades, shall help me.' " [1] She leads Wilhelm to a tree on a hill and says, " 'Here, . . . beneath this German tree, will I disclose to you the history of a German maiden . . . ,' " [2] then she begins to tell her story.

The long account of Hawthorne's gradual move, somewhat against his wish to control, toward *style indirect libre* is the story of his restricted development as a novelist. It is hardly an exaggeration to claim that he never advanced beyond what he knew intuitively at the writing of *Fanshawe,* a statement that may be taken, however, as attesting to his greatness, since he accomplished so much so early.

Even if his characters are distant, Hawthorne's style displays awareness from the beginning. In *Fanshawe,* Ellen's consciousness, Walcott's deductive ability, and Fanshawe's intuition are examples of an ability even in this early work to make characters aware of one another. The author's intimacy, however, is for the most part with Ellen; he tries, self-consciously, to remain detached from Fanshawe, with whom one would expect him to identify himself. But though Hawthorne seems capable of revealing Ellen's thoughts, he restrains himself. As Ellen speculates about the stranger who tried to speak to her, "her imagination was inclined to invest [him] with an undue singularity. It was, however, sufficiently unaccountable, that an entire stranger should venture to demand of her a private audience; and she assigned, in turn, a thousand motives for such a request, none of which were in any degree satisfactory. Her most prevailing thought, though she could not justify it to her reason, inclined her to believe that the angler was a messenger from her father. But wherefore he should deem it necessary to communicate any intelligence, that he might possess, only by means of a private interview, . . . was a mystery she could not solve" (III, 359). The sentence beginning "But wherefore . . ." culminates a movement that has gradually reached the point where it can turn to inner monologue; instead, there is but intimate, sympathetic description.

As Ellen rides away with Butler, she feels herself "completely in his power; and with that consciousness, there came a sudden change of feeling. . . . A thousand reasons forced themselves upon her mind, seeming to prove that she had been deceived; while the motives, so powerful with her but a moment before, had either vanished from her memory, or lost all their efficacy. Her companion . . ." (III, 431). Each of the first and third sentences could lead either into inner monologue or out of the mood altogether. Still, though he does not use the inner monologue, Hawthorne, even at this age, handles the description very deftly, and one has to conclude that he chose not to let his next sentence lead him away from the detachment. Comparison of this method with the use of asides in the *Marble Faun* clearly shows that he always controlled. In short, in this youthful work, Hawthorne was a very capable writer. He might justly have regretted the failure to let these characters come alive in such a manner as to match the imputations of awareness that appear so frequently, but he obviously refused to do so, when doing so was the easier thing to do. Instead, he simply keeps them away from their minds.

Even in the best of the tales that follow this early work, Hawthorne does not show the awareness of the inner monologue that he shows in *Fanshawe*. "Ethan Brand" and "Young Goodman Brown," where the chance for depth seems greatest, are of course allegorical. Technically, Goodman Brown is, paradoxically, but an unaware representative figure despite his appearance in a tale that deals explicitly with the moment of awareness. And in these stories Hawthorne continues to describe the thoughts. Goodman Brown's thoughts are set in quotation marks, for the most part. The one or two possible bits of monologue, since they are not in quotation marks, are probably the author's figures of speech. "The young man sat a few moments by the roadside, applauding himself greatly, and thinking with how clear a conscience he should meet the minister in his morning walk, nor shrink from the eye of good old Deacon Gookin. And what calm sleep would be his that very night, which was to have been spent so wickedly, but so purely and sweetly now, in the arms of Faith! Amidst these pleasant and praiseworthy meditations . . ." (II, 96). The possibility of an ironic tone in the contrast between "wickedly" and "purely and sweetly" makes one wonder if the author has intruded or if he unawarely is self-conscious.

Later, at the high point of the initiation ceremony, Brown "could have well-nigh sworn that the shape of his own dead father beckoned him to advance, looking downward from a smoke wreath, while a woman, with dim features of despair, threw out her hand to warn him back. Was it his mother? But he had no power to retreat one step . . ." (II, 102). There is a beautiful economy in the description, but the question appears more like a method of being ambiguous than like the thoughts of Goodman Brown. The same is true of the passage (II, 104) in which Hawthorne asks whether the basin contains water or blood.

Usually, these passages that are debatably interior monologue are questions that show a culmination of thought. They reveal the ultimate difference between the character's thought and the author's narrative without being either. The question seems to need to be answered in order to make the account quite *style indirect libre*. "Would he go? Yes, he would," is as far as third-person narration can go. If the next line replies with some such statement as, "He would indeed go," or, "Yes, he would do it," then one is dealing directly with the character. The handling of "Young Goodman Brown" shows no more personal relationship between narrator and character than exists in "The Haunted Mind," wherein Hawthorne writes, presumably, a depersonalized account of his own experience; or in "A Select Party," wherein he literally describes the fantasies of a man of fancy and is so impersonal as merely to describe allegorically from within the imagination. Despite an awareness of the technique of inner monologue and the early approach to its use, Hawthorne makes no real use of the technique until near the end of his career. Rejection of it kept him detached from the minds of his characters and left his characters perceptibly less than "round."

One might almost show that development in Hawthorne's tales gradually leads inevitably to the novels. In the tales the moment of awareness, at first associated somewhat ritualistically with a representative man, becomes, in the novels, associated with a figure who is developing consciousness. Most of the outstanding figures before Feathertop do not display consciousness in their actions. Their movements, thoughts, and feelings are narrated. The figures are made both to act and to have thoughts. This is true even of Reuben Bourne, who suffers much from feelings of guilt, and of the man of adamant, who ought to show an intense inner life. Perhaps Wakefield dimly realizes his situation. A step later in the development, Feathertop thoroughly realizes himself, yet without a real consciousness. At last "Rappaccini's Daughter," though not quite the last tale, chronologically, shows characters in interrelationships. Hawthorne has not previously done this. He did in *Fanshawe*, that is, and then dropped the technique. In "Rappaccini's Daughter," there is interaction in which more than one person is aware or is made aware.

The story of Beatrice and Giovanni deals with persons very sensitively conscious of each other. And this also is the case in the *Scarlet Letter*, where the three main characters have their moments of awareness. Dimmesdale and Chillingworth have been mentioned. One or two passages in which Hester appears might be called *style indirect libre*, but they are hardly more intimate than similar passages in "Young Goodman Brown" or *Fanshawe*. They are discussed in chapter 8. For the most part, the technique used with Hester is in the line of description that reaches its height in the handling of Hepzibah.

The tone of the portrayal of Hepzibah in the first pages tends to be ironic, in keeping with the manuscript references to her as the old maid. "The new shopkeeper dropped the first solid result of her commercial enterprise into the till. It was done! The sordid stain of that copper coin could never be washed away from her palm . . ." (III, 70). A passage of several pages at the beginning of chapter xv shows Hawthorne's intimate sympathy with Hepzibah's feelings, however, and it is one of the best of its kind. Characters and author both have become human, and the author is thoroughly in control of his material. "Never before had Hepzibah so adequately estimated the powerful character of her cousin Jaffrey. . . . For what, in the grasp of a man like this, was to become of Clifford's soft poetic nature, that never should have had a task more stubborn than to set a life of beautiful enjoyment to the flow and rhythm of musical cadences! . . . Was there no help, in their extremity?" (III, 287–89)

The longer passage contains numerous subtleties, ranging between simple description and what appears really to be inner monologue. Yet, the touch of mere rhetoric at the end, "Oh, the temptation! To make of his ponderous sorrow a security! To sink, with its leaden weight upon him, and never rise again!" (III, 294) makes one think that other brief passages also are but figures. In any case, though the passage as a whole is beautifully composed, one thing at least is wrong: this is not really Hepzibah thinking. The prose is too obviously set, and too much like the style of the rest of the book, to distinguish Hepzibah. Her mind is far more distraught than the prose. The method is not greatly different from that of the lengthy funeral oration upon Judge Pyncheon, except that the oration uses a good deal of irony.

The *Marble Faun* is third-person narration with occasional use of the first-person plural. The technique used is the formal dramatic aside, set in quotation marks that distinctly show the passage to be the thought of the characters, as if they actually talked to themselves. This method, and the long descriptions of thought and action, keep the narrator detached and unacquainted with his characters. Only the scene in which Hilda makes her confession approaches inner monologue, "And, ah, what a relief! When the hysteric gasp, the strife between words and sobs, had subsided, what a torture had passed away from her soul! It was all gone; her bosom was as pure now as in her childhood. She was a girl again; she was Hilda of the dovecote; not that doubtful creature whom her own doves had hardly recognized as their mistress and playmate, by reason of the death-scent that clung to her garments!" (vi, 407) But the person talking here is, unfortunately for his critics, Hawthorne.

In his last work, then, Hawthorne still shows no development toward such realistic handling of character as inner monolgue provides. Though the *Marble Faun* shows characters very much aware of one another, techniques are designed to maintain distance between author and character. Too, the dialogue between Hester and Dimmesdale in the forest is more intimate than either dialogue or asides in the *Marble Faun*. In the *Scarlet Letter* Hawthorne had prevented intimacy by keeping the characters apart, though the technique emphasizes awareness when they come together. In the *Marble Faun* he shows characters more often together, but he does not come so close to getting into their minds.

But, finally, in the last fragments, Hawthorne does establish that close sympathy with a character that involves the use of inner monologue. Here, perfectly anticipating James in using the single character to inscribe point of view, his narration is for the most part confined to what Redclyffe knows. Hawthorne does not attempt to show the thoughts of the other characters, and what one knows of them depends upon what Redclyffe observes. This technique was anticipated in the *Blithedale Romance,* where, however, the first-person narration automatically dispenses with the question of inner monologue.

Point of view has many facets in the fragments, including asides, musing that combines memory and the current of thought, very sympathetic and intimate description of thought, and shades of discourse too numerous to mention. The whole tone differs from most of what Hawthorne has previously written. Frequently, the description appears to make a subtle move into the character's mind.

The following passage will show some of the subtleties. Redclyffe, here called Etheredge, stands in the hall. "He wondered whether, in that fire, was the continuance of that custom which the Doctor's legend . . . spoke of . . . in expectation of the wanderer's return. It might be so, although the climate of England made it a natural custom enough, in a large and damp old room, into which many doors opened. . . . Was he himself—in another guise, as Lord Braithwaite had been saying—that long unexpected one? Was his the echoing tread that had been heard so long through the ages—so far through the wide world—approaching the bloodstained threshold?" [3]

The style here too makes use of questions. The following passage from the *Ancestral Footstep* begins with a question and then apparently moves into *style indirect libre.* "What right had he—an American, Republican, disconnected with this country so long, alien from its habits of thought and life, reverencing none of the things which Englishmen reverenced—what right had he to come with these musty claims from the dim past, to disturb them in the life that belonged to them? There was a higher and a deeper law than any connected with ancestral claims which he could assert; and he had an idea that the law bade him keep to the country which his ancestor had chosen and to its institutions, and not meddle nor make with England. The roots of his family tree could not reach under the ocean; he was at most but a seedling from the parent tree. While thus meditating . . ." (xi, 475). Or if this is not *style indirect libre*, Hawthorne never used the technique. And in a revision, he might have changed the style to achieve more detachment. The point is only to show what he does with point of view. Identification with the hero of the fragments is intimate, and the intimacy may be sufficiently uncomfortable for Hawthorne to cause him to change to the far different style and tone of the *Dolliver Romance*. He has anticipated the realistic technique of James but has persistently refrained from using it for characterization.

Yet, very little development occurs in Hawthorne's technique of characterization. More studied characterization occurs, of course, in the novels, and to some extent in what may be called the transition story of Beatrice. But, as indicated by Holgrave and Kenyon, Hester, Miriam and Zenobia, even when Hawthorne characterizes for novels he uses types though some are perhaps of his own devising. Hepzibah possibly escapes being a type. Hester does, one may claim, by being the first of Hawthorne's passionate women, though Catherine, mother of the gentle boy, anticipates her. Hilda first appears as Ellen and then as the sweet girl in all of Hawthorne's new couples.

Hawthorne is more interested in the personality of a ghost than in that of a person. He draws masks on shadows. Then he studies such types as the cold hearted man. Finding himself involved with the new character and new approach to character in Redclyffe, he must have realized what he had missed during all those years of writing. And he possibly feared getting into the minds of his characters. He may well have known that a character would usually be a projection of the author, despite any attempt to conceal autobiographical elements; in addition is the possibility that he never had any intention of trying to create a character. The plethora of moving shadows, the allegorical figures, the puppet shows; Hawthorne's ability to transform his material, and his great capacity as an artist all indicate that he usually and in general turned things out as he conceived them, intentionally substituting masks for characters.

It may have been Redclyffe's superior awareness that caused so much trouble in the composition of the later novels. Hawthorne had never before been confronted with so much strength and individuality—not in Hester nor in Miriam, not in any of his strong-minded women. They all had strength but not much self-awareness. In the *Ancestral Footstep*, probably for the first time, Hawthorne was dealing fully with himself, without concealing or projecting, and when this became clear to him he simply refused to write and reveal more. Also, as he indicates by the frequent interpolations of notes, perhaps he simply did not know where to go with the style that was developing as he worked.

But the point is the problem of self-awareness on the part of the character himself, whatever he is. Hawthorne almost consistently refuses to allow self-awareness. Hester's consciousness is never quite real, in part because one learns almost incidentally what goes on in her mind, even when she concludes that she ought not to have made the promise to Chillingworth not to reveal his identity. In addition, she is infrequently allowed to speak. In the scene of Dimmesdale's return from the forest, Hawthorne refuses to identify with his character when he obviously sympathizes with him in every respect, including perhaps Dimmesdale's vanity and sense of efficiency in wishing to end with the election-day sermon. The same is true of Hepzibah; Hawthorne provides but a rich description of her mind, without irony. Curiously, in his earliest work, Hawthorne promised more of development than he ever allowed himself until he suddenly made use of his abilities in the fragment of the *Ancestral Footstep*, where he first creates a full character, whom he then rejects, through a series of what he considered mishaps, to settle finally on Dolliver, a character that he had anticipated long before in Melmoth of *Fanshawe*. Hawthorne never made full use of his ability to characterize, and he was very much aware of having the ability. By means of techniques of narration that restrain and control his characters, as well as by the use of shadows and types, he detaches himself from intimacy. He does so by choice, ignoring techniques that would allow a depth of communication between the reader and the characters.

THE FIGURES in Hawthorne's early stories are used to represent the personal experience abstracted to a mythic level. These include Goodman Brown and Mr. Hooper. Gradually, these figures are replaced by others that are used for studies of human nature and for more specific studies of human beings and of character. Whereas the earlier stories may have been influenced by Greek tragedy, these works, such as "Egotism; or, the Bosom Serpent," are in the comic tradition, suggesting that Hawthorne may have experienced a change that led away from idealism to a sardonic, Jonsonian outlook. Despite their rarely optimistic subject matter, in general the early stories are phylogenic, mythic, and idealistic. The stories of the Manse period are analytic, concerned with types, manners, and morals; pessimistically involved with human action instead of human psychology. They deal with immediate and realistic material even if they are allegories. Hawthorne has seen the futility of the metaphysical and mythic concerns. He has lost his fresh perception through a gradual process of disillusionment in his own life. "Young Goodman Brown" probably records a sudden revelation that was a part of the process.

At some point during the attempts at the novel fragments, Hawthorne writes a hastily worded note that goes far to explain the experience of Young Goodman Brown. "Traditions of the temptation—the Divine used to have to go into the Forest and meet the Devil, and his wizard ancestor, and how his whole life was a struggle thereby, and his death troubled." [1] The note explains why Brown obviously knows his own purposes to be evil. He does not sleep and dream. He only walks imperceptibly from the edge of the forest deeper into the forest itself, from one *coulisse* to another.

Of course the experience is genuine, unreal as it may be. Hawthorne brilliantly tells the truth about traduced innocence; in short, it is the truth about the nature of things. But he may have designed a story to illustrate the point. Only Brown has the experience, despite what he thinks he sees of the others in the forest. No other is changed. And Hawthorne, by design or by ill design, forces the reader to be somewhat literal. For unless the whole story is dream or allegory, Brown himself is real and does have an experience that changes his entire life. He gains insight, if the doctrine of the story is valid, yet his insight is an exaggeration of the truth.

Brown's confrontation reveals the secrets to be full-bodied; and instead of leading him to place in society, this secret knowledge isolates him from society, making him too strongly aware. It is not valid to allow the devil's discourse on the human heart and the universal sin to conceal other aspects of the story. Hawthorne is more concerned with the experience than he is in propounding the Calvinistic doctrine of depravity.

Seeking the good of course is not human, nor is it human to find the good. And knowledge is not of the secrets of the ethical life but of sin. It is the devil's knowledge that destroys Goodman Brown, and the suggestion is that God shows only innocence to man, as He first did in Eden before one ate from the tree of knowledge. That is, God may have done man a great service in ordering him not to eat of the tree. On the other hand, if God may have concealed from man that evil existed, He may not have done a service; or at least man may feel Him to have deceived.

Identity is what Brown finds out—about everyone else first, with the inescapable conclusion that what he learns also is true of him. The story deals with more than a temptation. Brown's sorrow derives from his knowledge of his identity as allegorized man. That is, he represents the young person's introduction into human ways. It is important that his innocence should derive from his youth. And what happens to Brown is that he discovers that everyone else has known by analogy about him what he thought was true of him alone and which he kept secret. His pride is narcissistic youthfulness, and he feels ravished, as a young man may when another points out to him that he is now grown up. It means a recognition of the flesh without any respect for it or for the sensitivity of feelings. Brown hoped to live all human processes apart. He simply does not like the idea that everybody is doing it. He does not wish to share the common misery. He does not wish to admit to being human or to sharing in the sins, shortcomings, and common humanity of mankind. He still thinks his own guilt to be innocence and he, like Hester, resents being caught guilty at innocence. He may also regret simply not having known what others knew. He would feel violated and would realize that life means continual violation. In this respect, ignorant as one may be of another, people know too much about one another.

Brown, then, as representative man, learns human identity—as much as can be known of what man is, and he is appalled by it. He gets the realization that Adam must have got just before he took fig leaves to cover an immense shame. Hawthorne maintains, perhaps, that this is what man knows of himself and this his natural reaction to such knowledge. A man is indeed appalled by self-awareness and by self-knowledge. One may suggest also that this was a personal experience and that it is one from which Hawthorne himself never recovered.

"Young Goodman Brown" has obvious parallels with Milton's *Paradise Lost*, as critics [2] have suggested. Though Hawthorne depends very little on *Paradise Lost*, Milton's account of the fall in Book IX may be the source of Hawthorne's concept of violation. As the devil does in "Young Goodman Brown," the serpent in *Paradise Lost* make Adam and Eve thoroughly aware of each other. A comparison of Milton's description of the conditions before and after the act is, as in "Young Goodman Brown," of a violent change in the characters. Milton presents the experience in terms of a recognition of lust, in addition to or in place of the innocent love that had existed beween Adam and Eve. Goodman Brown and Faith must have had a similar recognition of the starkest nudity of human nature, though one has to remember that the experience tells only on Brown.

It needs emphasizing that Brown discovers both that he knows and knows that he knows and, in addition, that everyone else has already known, even Faith. Thus, his former innocence derived from ignorance. Knowledge comes with so much intensity that he is not able to excuse himself for the ignorance that he had. And he blames everyone else because none of them told him before. In short, he wants to have had divine knowledge, and he thus challenges the way of things in every respect. In addition, the devil's knowledge of evil reveals that acts of apparent innocence can subtly become evil. Worse, an act that is in fact innocent can be called evil. Things can be labeled sins—by the mind that makes a hell of heaven, or by an ethical code that condemns quite normal and natural acts. There, after all, is the trouble for Brown. But Hawthorne is not by any means following Milton's theology. Brown resents both the depraved act and the possibility that depraved individuals can think innocent acts depraved.

"The Minister's Black Veil" takes up another facet of the matter of self-knowledge. The minister's veil may symbolize the existence of secret guilt in everyman, but neither explicitly nor primarily that. An author who uses the face, as Hawthorne does, to characterize and as a means by which associates recognize character, now writes a story in which the face of the main character is concealed. The reader does not see the minister's face, and what it may have revealed to others before the veil was put on is never said. The situation leaves character to be determined by action alone. The minister isolates himself from society; his power for sympathy and understanding develops fully despite the isolation, as Hester's does, which makes it doubtful that Hawthorne proposes social integration, and the minister becomes in at least one sense a more integral part of society than he was before he began to wear the ambiguous veil.

The question of simple identity arises at the beginning of the story when someone asks the sexton, " 'Are you sure it is our parson?' " (1, 53) The sexton is sure; but though figure and name may be identified, nothing more is sure. Though it is Mr. Hooper, it is a new man. The people would expect to find another man behind the veil. And though Mr. Hooper is different he is yet Mr. Hooper, whatever that may mean. The complexities mount up; for it is likely that Mr. Hooper realizes all this. And at first his actions are misjudged. Afterwards he is judged by each according to his own sin or sorrow. That is, what Mr. Hooper comes to be depends on the particular sin or shortcoming of those who observe him. He is the perfect chameleon, which the narrator of "Night Sketches" says that he will not himself become, though he may sympathize with humanity. Mr. Hooper's sympathy is such that he seems to be whatever someone else imagines him to be, as if he chose not to be himself.

Hawthorne's ambiguity suggests that a mystery exists which is not to be divulged, but perhaps he only suggests the difficulty involved even in seeing what the problem is. That is, the secrets about what one essentially is, and the concern about them, may be mistaken for sin or sorrow. Most would mistake the symbol. Mr. Hooper would accomplish little, however, by telling his congregation what he knows. It would be, fundamentally, a matter of telling them what he does not know. There is little to be accomplished in assuring everyone that one is a miraculous being only half aware of oneself, whose origins and whose end are mysterious. But this is what Mr. Hooper knows really, and when he puts on the veil he has come to that realization. He has, in short, achieved a kind of wisdom or had an intuition, and he represents all this by the veil. The veil is somewhat like the whiteness of the whale. It symbolizes all ignorance of what really is—suggests that mysteries exist. But there is no great revelation either behind the whiteness or behind the blackness. Mr. Hooper might have said that he was a miracle without dramatizing it. Yet, perhaps the mystery of being is worth some hint of drama. In the incident with the mirror, Hawthorne dramatizes the minister's realization of how much of himself he hides, unintentionally, and of how much is hidden from him. He sees, in short, how much the veil covers. More than likely, too, it is another fig leaf, covering what Adam and Goodman Brown learned: the nakedness of being.

Hawthorne suggests that everything—every face and the earth itself—wears a black veil. There is always the question for the minister as to whether he sees through his own veil or always faces the veils that others wear. More likely, there is always a double veil. There is always illusion. There is a limited point of view from which every person observes. On the other side of every man's veil is the mask, image, or effect of every other man. What is true of men is true also of nature, of the whole of nature, of all things. There would always be at least two veils over things, and they cannot be removed at death.

The "sad mysteries" that we hide may be what we know of ourselves, things we are timid about and things that cannot be said or shown, such as the depths of love or sorrow. The veil, though it covers but the face in Hawthorne's tale, throws its influence over the whole person. The minister hides nothing. He only wears the symbol of all that is concealed. He never sees his own face either.

With "Young Goodman Brown" and "The Minister's Black Veil" Hawthorne is making some of the reflections that led him to the portrayal of such a figure as Hollingsworth and to the conclusion that every person is distorted in some manner because of his limitations and thus because of what he is. It is a conclusion that leaves one sad if he is an idealist. One's only solution is to develop a respect for the shortcoming, which, however, Hawthorne may never have been able to do.

The minister's veil conceals identity, then, not secret

guilt, unless one chooses, as of course he may legitimately, to say that a part of this hidden identity is that particular relationship between man and God that goes under the complex of original sin. One may claim indeed that the search for identity and individuality is original sin, while the unpardonable sin is tyranny over the identity of another. Both are violations. Knowledge of identity is forbidden since all secrets would be revealed if someone knew himself. Secret knowledge is knowledge of the self. The awareness it provides is godlike, what was forbidden to Adam.

Another aspect of the matter of knowledge and identity appears in "My Kinsman, Major Molyneux," which seems like an adept reconstruction of a dream. The wandering, the half-light, the houses, and the parade of persons are valid dream symbols, even if one is not sure what they mean. And as in a dream, the problem is the interplay between distortion and perception. Hawthorne may intend to say that the same thing is true of life.

The time is certain. "It was near nine o'clock of a moonlight evening . . ." (III, 617). Artificial light is required. As a pleasant bit of technique, the ferryman's raising his lantern allows the narrator to describe Robin, in rather unusual detail. Among his characteristics, Robin has "bright, cheerful eyes . . ." (III, 617), and both what he sees and what he seeks are to be important. And though his quest is ironically successful, what he sees will, for the most part, only complicate the quest. Robin in some measure resembles both the Red Cross Knight in the temple of pleasure and Dante in Hell without a guide.

Face and eye, looking and preceiving, are really over-emphasized. Always in the half-light, Robin must frequently adjust his vision from the light of the moon to the red glare from a doorway. The language in such words as "scrutinizing," "preceive," "discerned," emphasizes the theme. The conflicting lights join Robin's youth and inexperience in preventing him from seeing. The moonlight reveals the outlines of buildings and figures, but a lantern or artificial light from within a house is required to show him detail, except that in a "street of mean appearance," his "keen glance detected a woman's" (III, 625) scarlet petticoat. The deceptive ways are easier to see.

The expressionistic promenade of figures emphasizes both their clothing and Robin's inspection of their faces. Dress is carefully noted, as it is in the *Blithedale Romance*. Robin's clothing is fully described, as well as that of the kind man. Preparation is made for the appearance of the fantastic dress of the war party, a parallel to that of the ill-attired group in the restaurant. Everything has a carnival effect, as if Hawthorne were writing a grotesque version of the story he proposed in the notebooks, "to represent life as a masquerade," in which a natural face would occasionally appear. And if he meant to do just that, he chose proper conditions in using the moonlit night and the clothing disguises.

Everything appears to be designed either to deceive Robin or to prevent him from learning. Within this framework, Hawthorne ironically comments on Robin's wisdom and shrewdness, and ends with a portrayal of his chastened disillusionment by the tar and feather scene. What else does the story need to be called except an allegory of life?

Robin's persistence, if not his wisdom, shows him the whereabouts of the person of his kinsman, if not of his kinsman's house—and the house was perhaps as important as the kinsman. But the being he finds is in no way similar to the one he sought, nor does he find the place he sought. After mistaking numerous places, rejecting some, and being deceived by the most unlikely, he finds there is no place. He may find one, says the kind man, but Robin is not apt to look again.

The story anticipates Kafka's *The Castle*, wherein anyone who is urged seems to have some kind of knowledge, or at least awareness of possibilities, but wherein most persons are but vaguely conscious of what the influences are. The procession calls a great many surprised inhabitants to their windows. Some who are to participate even ask directions of Robin, ironically mistaking him for a man of knowledge. Enlightenment, not knowledge, is what Robin acquires in the night, after numerous dreamy scenes of confusion, as if, by questing, he were intended to reach some kind of goal. Fate promises to provide him with some kind of experience that ends in awareness, if he puts himself in the way of events.

The curious scene in which the procession halts in front of Robin anticipates the first scaffold scene in the *Scarlet Letter*. Mr. Hooper too was the center of attention, but in Robin's case a scene is devised in which everyone with whom he had contact faces him and laughs. In other cases the point is fairly clear: Hester's being is nude; Miriam's character is analyzed. But Robin is only viewed, faced by all those who knew how naïve he was. Goodman Brown had a similar experience. And that perhaps is enough, simply to have one's ignorance recognized and to have one's innocence considered guilt. This is Adam bare before God.

Hawthorne often seems on the point of calling up an underground man. Perhaps in "Wakefield" he did so, in his own way, without showing the sensitive consciousness in the character himself. The story derives from a study of motives: "What sort of a man was Wakefield?" (1, 154). He is ordinary and unpredictable, which means that he is human. A great novel might have resulted from the materials that Hawthorne crowds into this foreshortened account. If the moralizing is ignored—probably even the remarks on place in society ought to be—the story appears significant.

Wakefield creates a double in the fact of his own past existence, then views his former self. This action is a variant of the theme of eternal life that Fanshawe, Septimius, and the youthful Hawthorne wished for. The mature Hawthorne may be commenting on the senselessness of such a wish. Neither of Wakefield's lives is impressive. He looks back on a mere vacancy at first, then on nothing. And he verifies the assertion that Hawthorne admonishes himself, in a marginal note, to make in *Doctor Grimshawe's Secret*: "Express strongly the idea that the shortness &c of life shows that human action is a humbug." [3] Wakefield has two chances of proving the point.

Wakefield, like Dostoevsky's hero, is motivated by whatever of irrationality causes the "indefinable gleam" that his wife observes when he glances back at her through the glass. And that explanation is as satisfactory as the excuse of the "iron tissue of necessity" (I, 160), which never explains anything. "A morbid vanity," Hawthorne finally decides rather by chance, "lies nearest the bottom of the affair" (I, 157). Vanity tempts Wakefield to try to acquire "immortality."

Hawthorne's ineffectual moralizing that appears so useless and so out of context is a fairly good indication that the story is a failure, though Hawthorne sometimes probably uses the moral only to give his story a point. But the potential was very great in anticipating so much that was to appear later in the history of literature. Wakefield suggests not only the parallel with Dostoevsky's underground man; he also recalls at least two contemporaries: Melville's Bartleby and Büchner's Woyzeck.

Both identity and knowledge are themes of "The Great Stone Face." The face somehow represents an ideal, and the people attempt to find an incarnation of it. What Hawthorne thinks of their attempts is indicated by their actions: "the people bellowed . . ." (III, 420). They misapprehend the characteristics of their ideal and allow various illusions to deceive them.

No matter how much is made of the story it seems important only because it can be contrasted with others that deal more impressively with similar themes. "Mrs. Bullfrog," though no more impressive, also deals with the search for an ideal. And both stories lead to reflection upon the relationship between character and perception, in the search for knowledge or truth. "Mrs. Bullfrog" satirizes what Ernest takes seriously. Both characters probably compromise, at least with ignorance. The fastidious and assured Mr. Bullfrog is deceived not only by his fiancée's disguise; he is deceived even more basically in that he conceives of the possibility of *his* knowing what the ideal is. Even if he had got his ideal, and not one in disguise, no one else would necessarily have considered him successful. A man may have many useless ideals, many conceptions not worth realizing. An ideal, and the search for it, may greatly distort a person. Hawthorne disapproved of the ideals of a good many diverse reformers. Recognition of the valuelessness of useless striving suggests that since no concept may be proved to consist of an ideal, no ideal is worth striving for. One considers what Ethan Brand searches for and with what intensity. This story too may be a satire, and it would be no particular surprise to learn that the abortive romance was a version of the *Blithedale Romance*, wherein everyone is distorted by his motives and by what he is.

Ernest is fatherless, but if he can be said to have found himself, another contrast occurs. For this is about the only case in Hawthorne's work in which a questing character meets with what he seeks or with a happier destiny than he hoped for. "Ethan Brand," therefore, seems entirely uncharacteristic, though perhaps not so false in its resolution as the *House of the Seven Gables* is. On the other hand, Ralph Cranfield in "The Threefold Destiny," finds a place, by an almost lugubrious compromise. Even the man of adamant, at the other extreme, has a preferable fate. Ralph in any case returns to anonymity, taking advice that may have come from the author of *Candide*. If the story of Ralph can be taken as an allegory of life—if Ralph comes back to simple nonexistence—the moral fits, "Happy they who read the riddle without a weary world search, or a lifetime spent in vain!" (1, 538).

Ernest and Ralph were lucky, perhaps. The man of adamant, another man posssessed, destroys himself. The traditional quest, in which the act was done for the society as a whole, has turned against society as a whole and become entirely individualistic. Richard Digby makes an anti-quest that ends in self-destruction, like Ethan Brand's.

In "Feathertop," Hawthorne's last sketch before the novels, a similar action occurs; a representative man thor-

oughly realizes himself and acts accordingly. Mother
Rigby, the Creator, is cynical in her boast; "I've made
many a puppet since I've been a witch, but methinks this
is the finest of them all.' " (II, 256). " 'I'll make a man of
my scarecrow,' " she adds, " 'were it only for the joke's
sake!' " (II, 257). The moral rôle of this jesting creator in
the scarecrow affair suggests a dim view of both man and
God.

Feathertop becomes the whole man, in a sense, with
full self-consciousness and full awareness of himself. He,
in short, realizes himself. "We almost pity him" (II, 276),
when he finds out the enigma that has deceived a good
many whom he meets. "He threw up his arms with an
expression of despair that went further than any of his
previous manifestations towards vindicating his claims to
be reckoned human . . ." (II, 276).

Returning home at once, Feathertop announces, " 'I've
seen myself, mother! I've seen myself for the wretched,
ragged, empty thing I am! I'll exist no longer!' " (II, 277).
And he disintegrates: "the rudely-carved gap, that just
before had been a mouth, still seemed to twist itself into a
despairing grin, and was so far human" (II, 278).
Hawthorne, as existentialist, finds more dignity in the
created than in the creator. His own existence, his own
being, is what Feathertop rejects, not merely the world
and the other Feathertops and straw men. Ethan Brand,
Goodman Brown, Wakefield, and other characters in
Hawthorne share Feathertop's experience.

These stories, in general, are studies of vague quests
made in a wide gray universe. If they were unsuccessful
quests, they ended unpleasantly; if they were successful
they ended in anonymity. The concern has been with
what man is and what his life is worth. The figures have
not particularly needed consciousness.

Hawthorne early complimented himself on his knowledge of character. But in the early work he deals with
idealized versions of himself or with vague journey figures
like Goodman Brown, the ambitious guest, and Robin.
These figures represent man generically, in opposition to

or in the hands of antagonistic forces—man versus life. After about 1840 Hawthorne began to study types, presupposing, apparently, that men fell into such categories. The types are philosophical abstractions for the study of human nature, possibly anticipated in "The Minister's Black Veil." In general, the study of types means that Hawthorne deals with the "humour" character, which he could have got from the long Theophrastan tradition that includes Jonson, Molière, and Balzac. The study of Hollingsworth, obsessed with an "over-ruling purpose" (III, 70), for the most part completes the general study of human nature, and Hawthorne went on, in the novels, to ask each character to identify himself.

The problem of characterization is introduced in "The Old Apple Dealer," which was published in 1843. Hawthorne finds the old man negative, "too much subdued for him to feel anything acutely" (II, 498), as he says of Gervayse, in "The Christmas Banquet," wherein the "cold" character is discussed. The detached observer, whom the dispassionate character recalls, does of course not make his first appearance here. "Sights from a Steeple," and "Night Sketches" mention him. He appears in Endicott, Dr. Heidegger and the artist of "The Prophetic Pictures," as well as in the Intelligence Officer and the lover of Sylph Etherege. There is a touch of the figure in Fanshawe. But the matter is now handled in such a manner as to suggest that Hawthorne feels himself to have made a discovery. At least he has something he wants to say, and he may have intended to have Roderick Elliston both say and show it in the proposed *Allegories of the Human Heart*.

"The Christmas Banquet" is one of the proposed works, and in it Roderick, the former egoist, tells of Gervayse Hastings, maintaining that his own experience has given him insight into the character of Hastings. Gervayse resembles the old apple dealer in being "a hopeless puzzle" (II, 322). In reply to Roderick's question, at the end of the story, as to his success with the portrayal of Gervayse, Rosina says that her perception of Hastings is "rather by

dint of my own thought than your expression." Characterization lacks "because the characteristics are all negative."
If Hastings "could have imbibed one human grief at the
gloomy banquet . . . ," he would not have been "on the
outside of everything . . ." (II, 346). A similar remark is
made of the old apple dealer (II, 501). Such diverse figures
as Goodman Brown and the curator of a virtuoso's collection are also examples of the dispassionate character. The
curator of a virtuoso's collection is described as "one of
the hardest and coldest" (II, 547) of men. Hawthorne's
male characters tend to be incapable of feeling and to be
unwilling to involve themselves with their fellow human
beings.

The remarks on difficulties of characterization here are
on the surface misleading. The character of Hastings
comes through just about as Hawthorne intended, about
as well as Ethan Brand does, to take an example of one of
the most outstanding figures. One represents indifference,
the other passion. Both are possessed, and each acts accordingly. The difference indeed is in action. One acts, one
does not. And since it is Hastings' character that he does
not act, Hawthorne portrays him quite well—as a moral
type, possessed of a "humour."

The account of Roderick Elliston's egotism reveals him
to be possessed of a "humour" too, "a monstrous egotism
to which everything referred"—though maladies he de-
tects in others are often only human foibles. Jealousy
deriving from egotism is Roderick's "humour," but others
have many varieties of "that crime, which constitutes their
respective individuality" (II, 309). The trouble is a
" 'diseased self-contemplation' " (II, 319), according to
Roderick.

There is likely some relationship between Roderick's
Egotism and Ethan's Idea. Ethan too is distorted, to the
point of madness. He is not characterized, except that he
is said to be in no way remarkable. What one knows of
Ethan's character is found in a page of description that
records the change from good to bad as he becomes obsessed. "Ethan Brand" could have been the lead story in

Allegories of the Human Heart. In any case, Ethan is, if also a Gothic villain, another of the negative characters, whom Hawthorne could not "get hold of."

Both Roderick and Ethan are examples of distorted identity, examples of those who are not themselves because of some Idea that possesses them. Such a statement of course suggests the possibility that Ethan, for example, was never himself, whatever that may have been. And when one begins to consider the subtle involvements of the matter, he concludes that there is no way of knowing anything about what a person is. Hawthorne knows about psychology and human nature, equivocal as he may be, but does not know what people are. He cannot understand them. He knows, however, that they are all distorted. The theory that he proposes in "Egotism" is that a disease or a distortion of some other kind is what constitutes individuality. When Hawthorne changed from the study of representative men to the study of types, from Goodman Brown to Roderick Elliston, he went from a study of the disillusioned to a study of the distorted.

Few of the characters are either successful or happy in the various quests they make. The quests are made in a macrocosmic background of the mental and the metaphysical. Everyman's relationship is somehow with the beyond. There is very little mundane search of any kind, and one is not impressed by any amount of searching for wealth or position. The search is often so nameless that it is only a predetermined longing. Odysseys are unfinished. Characters do not know what they want or what they are here for. They want to be the other self in some fashion. However, the challenges they offer to the universe are, with a few exceptions, only the challenge of dissatisfaction. This of course implies criticism, for indeed they are not happy.

"RAPPACCINI'S DAUGHTER" deals with the enigmatic being
of the daughter of the scientist Rappaccini. The theme is
knowledge. The study of Beatrice occurs within a context
broadened by the question of what Giovanni's perception
can reveal of truth, a matter that is further broadened by
the antithesis between empiricism and reason as represented by the two doctors Rappaccini and Baglioni. Giovanni may at some point have been intended as the main
character, since he resembles the numerous young men in
Hawthorne's work who are disillusioned by some experience; but his rôle as it develops in the story is to inscribe
point of view, until, near the end, the author abandons
him. Thus, the conflict between Baglioni and Rappaccini
is important in so far as it affects Giovanni's perception of
Beatrice. The fact that he is also an actor in the affair
somewhat complicates his rôle as observer. It means of
course that, as in the case of any observer, what he sees
depends upon what he is. Giovanni is a human actor. He
is more involved than Coverdale and may have served as a
warning to him. Giovanni is even more limited than Coverdale because he is blinded by his lust for Beatrice. The
story displays not the doctrine of isolation that
Hawthorne lamely draws on near the end but the violation of Beatrice that occurs during the attempt to divine
what she is and subsequently change her, an attempt
made by all three male characters. This is Hawthorne's
first real success at showing characters quite aware of one

another, as he briefly did in stories like "The Birthmark" and "Sylph Etherege," and here, as in those stories and in the novels, interrelationships lead to violations. Rappaccini "poisons" Beatrice and Baglioni "cures" her. Both acts are violations of her essential being. Aside from this, their rôles are confined to such machinations as Rappaccini may be engaged in and to such contact as exists between Giovanni and Baglioni. The motives of the two doctors apparently derive to a considerable extent from the two approaches to science. Baglioni represents the Aristotelian deductive approach that speaks of the " 'arcana of medical science' " (II, 125). Rappaccini is the new empiricist. Giovanni and Beatrice are caught in the conflict, wherein Giovanni concentrates more specifically on determining what Beatrice is. He violates her both by the prying and by the attempt to change her.

The themes of knowledge and observation are emphasized in the language by the many words that refer to observation and perception. Light and day are associated with clear thinking. When Giovanni opens the window to look into the garden "which his dreams had made so fertile with mysteries," the sun has "brought everything within the limits of ordinary experience" (II, 115); except, of course, that he makes a mistake. His fanciful observations in the moonlight had provided him with a truer view. Now his "ordinary experience" of the past has only an adverse effect upon his perceptive ability. In short, and in very earnest, traditional methods of perception, like traditional methods of logic and investigation, are not sufficient. They only generate confusion. Giovanni's conclusion is ironic. "Neither the sickly and thoughtworn Dr. Giacomo Rappaccini, it is true, nor his brilliant daughter, were now visible; so that Giovanni could not determine how much of the singularity which he attributed to both was due to their own qualities and how much to his wonderworking fancy; but he was inclined to take a most rational view of the whole matter" (II, 115).

From this point on, the story is concerned with the developing intensity of awareness between the two main characters. Beatrice's naïveté, her consequent naturalness of action, which will continue even as she comes to love Giovanni, is contrasted with Giovanni's intimate and lustful awareness of her. And the deepening mystery that runs concomitantly with Giovanni's awareness will make him eventually utter the question that so many of Hawthorne's characters address to or about one another: " 'What is this being? Beautiful shall I call her, or inexpressibly terrible' " (II, 120)? When the question later comes up between them, Beatrice cautions Giovanni against believing rumors and says, " 'Believe nothing of me save what you see with your own eyes' " (II, 129). Ironically, however, he does, for the most part, judge her by what he sees, and he recognizes possible deception, " 'And must I believe all that I have seen with my own eyes? . . .' " Beatrice "looked full into Giovanni's eyes, and responded to his gaze of uneasy suspicion with a queenlike haughtiness." Then she says, " 'Forget whatever you may have fancied in regard to me.' " Pointing up the dichotomy between truth and perception, she adds, " 'If true to the outward senses, still it may be false in its essence; but the words of Beatrice Rappaccini's lips are true from the depths of the heart outward. Those you may believe' " (II, 129–30). She now appeals to a sense easier deceived in Giovanni, already so, since apparently his five senses are not deceived. And, as it happens, precisely the sense Beatrice appeals to, his heart, is somehow being deceived.

The poison in Beatrice actually seems to be a part of her. It influences her actions. She is aware of it. Embarrassed with the knowledge, she shields her father and is at first equivocal to Giovanni. Does she not know that he too is being poisoned? She shields him from the touch of the plant itself. She is genuine enough to die for him. But she cannot be judged by what one sees, nor easily by her actions, it seems. She finally can be judged only by what she says. Yet, she has also spoken equivocally.

Giovanni, convinced of his own knowledge or not, says to Baglioni, " 'You know not the Signora Beatrice,' " to which Baglioni replies, " 'I know this wretched girl far better than yourself. You shall hear the truth . . .' " (II, 137). And Giovanni learns precisely what he has known, in one sense. Yet, he too is right, as it turns out. They both are, but each knows only a portion of the truth about Beatrice. There are two sides at least to her being, whatever may be her character. " 'It is a dream,' " says Giovanni, which Baglioni echoes in his way by suggesting that Beatrice may be brought again " 'within the limits of ordinary nature,' " recalling Giovanni's thought of "ordinary experience," and both remarks reflecting a paradox in the application of "ordinary" to either nature or experience. Baglioni emphasizes the problem again in contrasting the "vile empiric" with " 'those who respect the good old rules of the medical profession' " (II, 138).

Now follows a page of all the faces of truth, the language burgeoning with such words as refer to seeing and being. Giovanni recalls all he first saw of Beatrice. "These incidents, however, dissolving in the pure light of her character, had no longer the efficacy of facts, but were acknowledged as mistaken fantasies, by whatever testimony of the senses they might appear to be substantiated. There is something truer and more real than what we can see with the eyes and touch with the finger. On such better evidence had Giovanni founded his confidence in Beatrice . . ." (II, 139).

Hawthorne very neatly gets it all in. Besides all these aspects of truth and knowledge and their opposites, the passage refers also to the nature of Giovanni's passion and his deception and to the ambiguity of Beatrice. Giovanni "resolved to institute some decisive test" (II, 139), taking the empiric approach. He thus will seek knowledge as forbidden as that sought by Rappaccini, and he will commit the same crime. Beatrice, the object of study for all, judged by their assumptions, perceptions, and confusion, may or may not prove herself in death. No one ever really knows anything about her. That, not isolation, is Giovanni's experience.

Shorn of its machinery, "Rappaccini's Daughter" seems basically like a dramatic treatment of an essay by the

eighteenth-century scientist Benjamin Rush [1] on the conflict between the two approaches to science, deduction
and induction. But what of the rest of the story, with its
unusual setting and its moral applied by tape and glue?
Though criticism somewhat irrationally tends to confine
Hawthorne's reading and perhaps his knowledge of literature to the list of books borrowed from the Athenaeum, it
seems not unlikely that when Oriental literature had great
currency among the intellectuals of Hawthorne's time, he
might have read some of it himself. "Rappaccini's Daughter" has several resemblances to Kalidasa's *Shakuntala,*
which Thoreau had read and might have recommended to
Hawthorne. For this story particularly, one would like to
know sources that were added to the usual themes of
knowledge and identity.

   "Rappaccini's Daughter" points up, in the particular
handling of the theme of knowledge, a possible characteristic of Hawthorne's use of language that may deserve
further study. As the material below on the *House of the
Seven Gables* indicates, Hawthorne uses a great many
words referring to aspects of mental activity. One gradually acquires the feeling that for Hawthorne every verb
defines some mental state of knowledge or ignorance,
quite specifically suggesting a momentary state of being,
more than is usually the case. That is, Hawthorne is not
merely careful in the choice of words or of verbs; he also
considers them as naming and describing what a character
is at a certain time as he has a certain experience. Thus,
Giovanni ponders, queries, reflects, experiments, decides,
investigates, puzzles, and—is confused. Even "love" and
"lust" are used to describe his mental activity, an activity
deriving from observation of the enigmatic figure of Beatrice and occurring in a framework that allows perception
to be distorted by emotion. In short, much of the problem
that Beatrice is for Giovanni results from what Giovanni
is. One sees, thereby, the numerous difficulties involved in
gaining knowledge about a human being and about being.

   Since Hawthorne very often repeated themes, it is not
surprising that "Rappaccini's Daughter" strikes one as

being, though unintended, a preliminary study for the novels. The *Scarlet Letter* investigates the secrets of Hester alone, but each of the other novels presents a strong female character and a weak one; though of course Hepzibah's age prevents anyone from being much concerned with any secrets she may have. Nevertheless, a pattern emerges that shows the exotic woman and her much simpler and less secretive double, in a technique matching Hawthorne's treatment of the men, who are presented with doubles and foils from Fanshawe on. On this analogy, and encouraged by some of the remarks that Beatrice addresses to the plant, one may assume that in "Rappaccini's Daughter" too Hawthorne has created the exotic sister of the pure young woman. The theme of Beatrice and her poisonous sister is repeated specifically in the *Marble Faun*, in Hilda's feeling that she has been contaminated by the contact with Miriam. Whether Zenobia would have felt that the threat from Priscilla was analogous to poison, one does not know. Yet the distinction holds. Both types apparently were threats to the men, however. The exotic sister kept men upset, by threatening to devour them by means of the eternal feminine. The other provided men with less excitement but in offering them surcease apparently used the eternal feminine to absorb them unawares.

ALL HAWTHORNE'S WORK is concerned with awareness. In general between *Fanshawe* and the *Scarlet Letter*, the concern is with a representative figure who has some kind of confrontation and subsequent revelation. His enlightenment reveals something about human psychology. In "Rappaccini's Daughter" characters are aware of one another, but the enigma is one-sided; Beatrice does not wonder who Giovanni is. In the novels, Hawthorne creates figures who exchange awareness of one another and interact. The *Blithedale Romance* shows Coverdale and Zenobia constantly aware of each other. Hilda in the *Marble Faun* is very nearly aware of herself, and, with Redclyffe, Hawthorne creates a figure entirely aware of himself. And awareness in part accounts for the greatness of the *Scarlet Letter*. Observation, identity, and knowledge are the themes.

The problem of knowledge is emphasized in the *Scarlet Letter* by expansive observation that reveals a broad scene of action but nothing conclusive about the action. "'. . . Mistress Prynne . . . [is] set where man, woman, and child may have a fair sight of her brave apparel . . .'" (1, 54), but no one ever understands what he sees of her. Rumor and superstition only emphasize the poles of curiosity and ignorance. Interpretation of Pearl, the clearest fact, is fraught with so much connotation that identity cannot be determined. While there is a mystery about which everyone is curious, the way of perceiving—

the framework of impressibility and superstition within which they perceive—urges them to explain the truth by easier illusions. Or, in short, they mask plain facts in equivocations. The exception to this apparently is Chillingworth, who, though he has not foreseen, now sees. Indeed, the actors in the drama, urged by the intuition of oversensitivity and distaught common sense, come to know their own conditions. But while sharpened intuition may give them some insight into one another and while the three main characters are supremely aware of one another even when they conceal awareness, there is doubt as to whether they are ever known to one another. In a story where so much is open, very little is known. And even when the reader sees that Dimmesdale is Hester's lover, he waits until the end for the proof, such as it is. Facts vanish, or else whirl in such winds as disperse their potency. The problem of knowledge is a perplexing one throughout the *Scarlet Letter*. Observation occurs within a framework of disbelief and superstition. As Hawthorne says, "When an uninstructed multitude attempts to see with its eyes, it is exceedingly apt to be deceived" (1, 127), a remark that has a potential not much affected, as the actions of Hawthorne's crowds show, by the immediately following sentence that credits the public with a warm heart. And identity is never certain.

Display and observation naturally center on the three outstanding scaffold scenes in the market place. The second, in which Dimmesdale displays himself only in the dark, unnoticed by all but Hester, Pearl, and Chillingworth, emphasizes the first and third, which appear to show too much. The lengthy opening of the book is an open display of Hester's being. The language is filled with references to all there is to see in the simple action of Hester's walk from the prison to the market place. The action is emphasized by the setting, a square cut out of the forest, a clear path going from the jail to the market place, a raised platform on which a live being huddles with a child, "displayed to the surrounding multitude . . ." (1, 56), and also observed from above by the numerous officials on the church balcony. The mere facts of what is seen are in every way, despite being ordinary, thoroughly startling.

Hawthorne's ability at showing the intensity of self-awareness without inner monologue appears in the passage that describes Hester's thought while she is on the scaffold. The description never quite makes Hester live, not even when, near the end of the scene, she realizes just where she is (1, 59). One is never quite sure that Hawthorne is not using romantic irony in these intimate passages. Still, the passage is remarkably good, in part because of the limits within which, despite the trace of irony, Hawthorne controls himself. The catalogue of memories is good technique. Hester's recollection of looking at herself in the mirror shifts to reveal the shadow of Chillingworth behind her in the glass. Here is both a description of him and a foreshadowing of his appearances as a figure of evil. Memory leads Hester chronologically, in another example of good technique, from her childhood gradually to the scaffold. And then comes a remarkable artistic stroke. Hester becomes quite thoroughly aware, naming her name, looking at "Hester Prynne,—yes, at herself,—who stood on the scaffold of the pillory, an infant on her arm . . ." (1, 58). "Could it be true?" she asked and then she "turned her eyes downward at the scarlet letter, and even touched it with her fingers, to assure herself that the infant and the shame were real. Yes!—these were her realities,—all else had vanished!" (1, 59).

This scene of self-awareness is followed immediately, in a chapter called "The Recognition," by an exchange of awareness with the shadow prefigured in the memory of the mirror reflection—Hawthorne doubles and redoubles shades and modes of perception—memory, mirror, reflection, recognition. Every detail of the exchange is recorded. Hester sees. Chillingworth sees—has seen. His face is described and his eyes. The narrative concentrates on what his face reveals—intelligence, careless glance, unawareness, concentration, awareness. There is an exchange of glances:

". . . he found the eyes of Hester Prynne fastened on his own . . . , saw that she appeared to recognize him . . . , made a gesture . . ." with his finger "and laid it on his lips" (1, 61). Hester sees him touch a bystander, and she knows that when they meet he will know thoroughly. Someone who knows her intimately sees her in the starkest nudity of being.

Awareness and observation are redoubled within and outside of the character. The townsman observes to Chillingworth that, " 'Peradventure the guilty one stands looking on at this sad spectacle, unknown of man, and forgetting that God sees him' " (1, 62). Now, to the repeated claim that this is Puritan justice, " 'where iniquity is dragged out into the sunshine' " (1, 54), is added Chillingworth's refrain, " 'But he will be known!—he will be known!—he will be known!' " (1, 63). The remark—the repetition—states the theme, summarizes the preceding action—all of it psychological—and characterizes Chillingworth. Evil searches out the truth comparably to the search Mephistopheles makes into the being of Faust, opposed only by Hester's nerve in her unaware assurance that her child will never know its father (1, 68).

The narrative briefly returns to Hester's cognizance, folding perception back on perception, to force intensity quite out of the bounds of language. Hester sees Chillingworth so fixedly that she is in a stupor—"all other objects in the visible world seemed to vanish, leaving only him and her" (1, 63). But even this recognition is preferable to their being alone, for ". . . she was conscious of a shelter in the presence of these thousand witnesses . . . [and] fled for refuge, as it were, to the public exposure . . ." (1, 63–64).

Much of the greatness of the *Scarlet Letter* derives from what it displays of one character's awareness not only of another but also of himself, and of the nudity of the situation wherein they meet. Hester is as thoroughly and desolately exposed as it is conceivable to be. Still, something lacks. These persons are too archaic to live. "The Interview" scene in which Hester and Chillingworth finally meet is less intense than the preceding scenes. Chillingworth now mixes dissimulation and cognizance as Hester gazes at him, pondering his intentions. He meets her awareness of him for the most part only in the directness of his speech. But the undercurrent of mutual awareness is evident when Hester replies to his hindsight and regret in saying " '. . . thou knowest that I was frank with thee. I felt no love, nor feigned any' " (1, 74). And as Chillingworth ends his lengthy speech with assurance that he will find out the lover, Hester feels nearly as if he sees the name in her mind. She takes the oath to conceal his identity, as Chillingworth resumes his cover of detachment and "refined cruelty."

Self-awareness is associated with changes in all three main characters. Hawthorne analyzes Chillingworth descriptively (1, 139) before showing him aware of the change that may have occurred in him. Hester notes the change seven years after (1, 169), and during the conversation with Hester, Chillingworth has "one of those moments—which sometimes occur only at the interval of years—when a man's moral aspect is faithfully revealed to his mind's eye" (1, 172). Recalling first what he had been as a humanist, he now calls himself "a fiend," and he finishes with a question: " 'Who made me so?' " (1, 173) that reverberates beyond the confines of the situation, going beyond Dimmesdale's sin to parallel the question repeatedly asked about Pearl: in effect, What is the source of being? His conclusion is that of a fatalist unable to tell: as he said of Dimmesdale's malady, earlier, " '. . . the disease is what I seem to know, yet know it not' " (1, 135).

But the great scene of awareness in the *Scarlet Letter*, in every respect the greatest scene in Hawthorne's work, is the meeting between Hester and Dimmesdale in the forest. Its effectiveness derives in part from the fact that it reveals so much awareness between characters who, despite their complicity, have during the action seemed unaware of each other. Hester and Dimmesdale, Hawthorne himself points out, are like spirits meeting for the first time after death—"Each a ghost, and awe-stricken at the other ghost! They were awe-stricken likewise at themselves; because the crisis flung back to them their consciousness, and revealed to each heart its history and experience, as life never does, except at such breathless epochs. The soul beheld its features in the mirror of the passing moment" (1, 190), and, one might add, each in the mirror of the other's awareness.

The height of feeling and awareness is in Hester's impassioned speech that comes just after the revelation that she still loves Dimmesdale. For the first time in the conversation or in the book, she uses his first name, " 'O Arthur . . . forgive me!' " Now, perhaps, and in what follows, in her insistence on being forgiven, one may believe Hester passionate. And Dimmesdale, less aware because of his illness perhaps and his egotism, his passionate nature not revealed until the expressionistic scene when he returns to the village, does forgive. This awareness is so intense that mentally they again commit their original sin, and Dimmesdale returns, the whole episode a version of "Young Goodman Brown," the priest tempted in the forest.

A conversation between Chillingworth and Dimmesdale points up one of the major themes of the *Scarlet Letter*: Who is Dimmesdale?—a question not of necessity related to that of Pearl's origin. Whether or not Hawthorne intended the *Scarlet Letter* to emphasize the need for showing one's worst to the view of others, he concentrates on what Dimmesdale is. Unfortunately, the opinions of both Chillingworth and Dimmesdale, in their discussion of the subject, may be more than usually personal. Dimmesdale's argument is that one can accomplish more by hiding such guilt as he may have, to which Chillingworth replies with a question: Can " 'a false show be better— . . . be more for God's glory, or man's welfare—than God's own truth?' " (1, 133). It is fundamental to his character that Dimmesdale should ponder his own being. Though he has not agreed with Chillingworth, he considers himself "a pollution and a lie" (1, 143). But Hester approves of what he is. She assures him, in the forest scene, that his " 'present life is not less holy, in very truth, than it seems in people's eyes' " (1, 191). Chillingworth's argument was devised to appeal to Dimmesdale's combination of sincerity and pride, and the latter's reply is one of practical action in the face of hopelessness. Whether since converted or not, Dimmesdale now, agreeing with Chillingworth's earlier argument, insists to Hester that his work is of no value. But even more interesting in view of Hawthorne's various comments on identity, he is glad now " 'to look into an eye that recognizes me for what I am!' " which he would, he says, ironically, be glad to have even a worst enemy do, though he condemns Chillingworth a moment later for doing so (1, 192–93). Hawthorne sees no end to the complexities. He has, however, recognized something fundamentally true about human psychology. Dimmesdale wishes to be thoroughly known by someone.

It is of course one intent of the action to discover Pearl's origins. First, Hester is exhorted by Mr. Wilson to reveal the identity and covertly by Dimmesdale to conceal it. Chillingworth also puts the question directly: " 'But, Hester, the man lives who has wronged us both! Who is he?' " (1, 75) —a remark echoed when Hester and Dimmesdale agree that Chillingworth has wronged them both. The lengthy chapter on Pearl is designed to increase the mystery. Her being is as mysterious as her origins. Climaxing the description of Pearl's oddities, Hawthorne makes Hester say, " 'O Father in Heaven,—if Thou art still my Father,—what is this being which I have brought into the world!' " (1, 96).

At the Governor's, Mr. Wilson attempts to catechize Pearl, " 'Canst thou tell me, my child, who made thee?' " (1, 111). And Pearl herself inquires, as Ned does of Dr. Grimshawe; then, much later, she tells the ship's captain that her father is said to be the "Prince of the Air" (1, 245), the remark that Mignon in *Wilhelm Meister* uses to reply to a similar question. It is far more than a question of who joined Hester in sin. Even Chillingworth seriously asks, of Dimmesdale, " 'What, in Heaven's name, is

she? . . . Hath she any discoverable principle of being?' "
(1, 134).

As Pearl grows up, the mysteries increase. Looking into
the "unsearchable abyss of her black eyes," Hester asks
Pearl, " 'Child, what art thou?' " (1, 97). And later in the
scene, replying to Pearl's insistence on being who she is:
" 'Tell me, then, what thou art, and who sent thee
hither?' " Pearl replies seriously, " 'Tell me, mother! . . .
Do thou tell me!' " (1, 98). Hawthorne makes too much
of Pearl, of course, yet beneath the fanciful clamor lies
the unanswerable questions of who Pearl is, what she is,
and what will become of her.

The search for Pearl's father is on two levels. Or perhaps there is, on one level represented by Chillingworth, a
search and, on the other represented by Pearl, the urge to
reveal. Amid all the observation, curiosity, and speculation
as to what clear facts may really indicate, Pearl at three
months hears the minister's voice and turns a "hitherto
vacant gaze towards Mr. Dimmesdale . . ." (1, 67).
Hawthorne's father-son theme is repeated here, with the
father's rejection of the child.

The identity of each of the characters must be determined. At the end of the second scaffold scene, when
Dimmesdale has first called Pearl and Hester to him, then
noticed Chillingworth, in a remarkable example of double
awareness and double ignorance, he turns to Hester and
says, " 'Who is this man, Hester? . . . I shiver at him!
Dost thou know the man?' " (1, 156). The question arises
from the deepest intuition of the threat of evil.
Hawthorne uses a variation of the Doppelgänger theme in
discussing Chillingworth, who "chose to withdraw his
name from the roll of mankind, and, as regarded his
former ties and interests, to vanish out of life as completely as if he indeed lay at the bottom of the
ocean . . ." (1, 118–19), as rumored. He is a variety of
Wakefield, another being who develops and lives his other
self. But the implication is not that these two have ceased
to communicate with mankind; instead, they avoid a part
of themselves, seeking anonymity.

The Chillingworth who appears in the dialogue is not a mere shade. There is realistic insight in the portrayal of him, once his studies of alchemy and Indian herbs are ignored. A mere touch of inner monologue, even so little as Hawthorne may use with Hester, to show something of the change, and of Chillingworth's realization of it, and there would be substance to go with the Chillingworth of the dialogue. As he wanders along the seashore just prior to the meeting with Hester, Chillingworth recognizes that he is no longer the gentle humanist that he was. Hawthorne may have been thinking of Iago, as he portrayed the figure of evil. But the scene fails to dramatize the realization and adds to Hawthorne's failure to develop the character of Chillingworth. Yet Chillingworth's fixing on Dimmesdale, his knowledge of Dimmesdale's character, his knowledge of Hester, and his intuition and awareness do not come merely from revenge and evil but from a realistic concept of character.

The real enigma in the *Scarlet Letter* is Hester, though she may be in one sense the one of whom the most is known. Chillingworth deceives the townsman in asking what he already knows, who Hester is, but is himself deceived in knowing much less of Hester than he thinks. True as Hester may be, sympathetic as the infliction may cause her to be with the troubles of others, an old theme in Hawthorne, she finally shows something of the passions that Hawthorne has attributed to her. And she does not tell the whole truth to Chillingworth in saying that the scarlet letter has done his work for him. Hawthorne takes a good deal of time to indicate that Hester has gradually come to be what he said she was—a freethinker. There seems to be little doubt that Hester is as good as people have come to believe her to be though little doubt that she was ever less good. She would again commit the act that condemned her, but she does not sin at either time, it seems. On one level, the sin is but called so by men, in time and place. On another level, it was an irrational act that did not really affect character but only actions. On still another level, the act is the contrary; it is a characteristic act, and all the action that follows is characteristic of Hester. Like Miriam and Zenobia, Hester is essentially good. One's attempts to judge her, like those of her contemporaries, are violations of being and wrong attempts to decide on what is true of her. Hester only is.

Hester provides also a good commentary on the matter of distortion of character, in the scene in which she sees her reflection in the suit of armor. One does not know Hawthorne's intention. Perhaps he means only to indicate that Hester feels as if the letter that distorts and covers her figure in the mirror pervades her being. But the incident also suggests distortion of character. That is, others perceive Hester as they do Roderick, as being one thing only. Her being is limited. She is not Hester, individual, composed of irrationalities, contraries, and passions, as persons are; instead, she is only a strumpet, adultress, or whatever is described by the word shouted by the Puritan children of an indelicate age. In short, just as the convex reflection distorts Hester's dress by covering her with the scarlet of the letter, so perception of her is distorted by perception of only one aspect of her character. And indeed there may be nothing displayed or perceived of her character. Instead, she is judged merely by one irrational and passionate act, by something perhaps quite uncharacteristic.

The people never come to know any of the characters. No one ever knows Hester. Dimmesdale is consistently misinterpreted. The crowds refuse to take any of his statements, not even his confession, at face value. Chillingworth never uses his own name and is known to Hester alone. Pearl has but a first name. On the other hand, the surface mysteries are revealed. If Pearl's actions are indicative, the action, both physically and psychologically, is resolved. But unfortunately, the end does not have the remarkable awareness of the beginning and of the book as a whole. Dimmesdale's last words are to the crowd, a rhetorical farewell. The end of the book is a confusing public display in which the characters have lost whatever individuality they had and merged with the throng.

In "The Procession" as Dimmesdale goes past, Hester muses, in a passage that is as close as Hawthorne ever comes to the inner monologue in this book, "One glance of recognition, she had imagined, must needs pass between them. She thought of the dim forest. . . . . . . How deeply had they known each other then! And was this the man? She hardly knew him now!" (1, 239). The question reflects their whole relationship as seen in the action. The action is such that when Hester, on the scaffold, recalls her past life, she does not recall the most intimate scene, the one that motivates the action as a whole. The age is too delicate. It is action in which Dimmesdale takes almost no note of his daughter or of Hester, not because he is hypocritical or callous but because they do not in fact know what they know of one another.

Only Chillingworth, the mask of the author, far removed perhaps, knows of them. They cannot be known to one another. They are innocent, in their loves, in their lives, and in their instincts. And there are no better examples in Hawthorne's work of figures manipulated on a scene that is intended to neglect the characters in order to display the interaction of forces bigger than life. If the *Scarlet Letter* is valid as Hawthorne's vision, human kind can have no hope. There may be something in recognizing the fact and preventing disillusionment, but nothing of more value. Dimmesdale and Hester, the innocent ones, have, under the artificial circumstances imposed by society, violated each other. Despite the attempt at a happy ending, there is no way out. The situation is as desolate as it is for Miriam and Donatello, for Hollingsworth and Priscilla. And the vision is as bleak as that of Schopenhauer and Sartre.

The *Scarlet Letter* is of course more than is suggested by the discussion of its use of themes of identity and knowledge. The existence of numerous interpretations indicates the difficulty one has in determining what the novel means. Possibly, at least this once when he was at the height of his career, Hawthorne could not form his content. There was an inundation of the mythic and

elemental that required either a longer or a shorter narrative. Longer, if all suggested material was to be formed,
and shorter if characters, action, and drama were to be
confined to description. One lack was a ritual setting, such
as "Young Goodman Brown" has. The historical novel
and the Puritan society were insufficient, at least as
Hawthorne used them. The impulse of the mythic was
evident from the beginning. When the narrator finds the
manuscript and the scarlet letter in the customs house, the
mythic has already exerted itself toward expression. The
letter is not merely scarlet but fiery with the intense
Medean passion of Hester. Yet, Hawthorne persistently
refuses to allow his own vision to guide him, and Hester
never really achieves the stature of her symbol.

Hawthorne combined two of his themes in the *Scarlet
Letter,* violation and the unknown. Hawthorne's interest
in the concept of violation led him gradually to concentrate on the unseen influence that caused violations of individuality. A great deal of the work that followed "Young
Goodman Brown" was plotted on the theme of the ma-
nipulating figure. The point was to display the force that
was motivating the action. Hawthorne realized of course
that he could not determine ultimate causes—what made
Chillingworth evil, for example. Certainly, he could not
determine the source of evil itself. Thus, he concentrated
on the intermediate and visible cause represented by the
figure of the manipulator. And he recognized of course
that behind the manipulator was the unknown. Man's
ignorance, in short, allows, perhaps creates, both potential
and chance in events. "David Swan" shows both
Hawthorne's speculation and the relationship between the
themes of violation and the unknown. David is representative man, and his known world is the world of human
knowledge. But there is a cosmos of unknown potential
outside David's awareness, and any human creature in the
known world may be a force of this unknown. Thus, while
David sleeps in ignorance of all the potential, he avoids
the chance for riches, love and death, unaware of both the
offers and the threat. Yet one or more of several agents

might have changed his life fundamentally, or even have taken his life. More of course may be said of fate, chance, and sleep, but these themes are presently aside from the subject. David's case is, however, that of every one. At times, as with the characters in the *Scarlet Letter*, persons come into contact with one or more of the forces that David avoided by being asleep.

Basically, then, the *Scarlet Letter* deals with the agent of the unknown who manipulates and destroys. Thus, Chillingworth is at the source of the action in the book, and one of the intentions was to show his manipulations of the other figures within the whole framework of the action. The motivating force contacts other forces, such as Dimmesdale's character and the Puritan background. All the conflicting and antagonistic forces then interact in response to the generating force. To judge from the other novels, Hawthorne had in mind to characterize the generating force sufficiently to show the strength and influence it exerted, but not enough to make the representative appear personally important. Or perhaps Hawthorne intended to devise quite distinct variants of the manipulator. Yet, Westervelt, Old Moodie, Holgrave, Doctor Grimshawe, and the Spectre of the Catacombs dominate the action while being relatively uninvolved in the drama. In many circumstances, and with another man, the interaction might end in resolution. Hawthorne, however, does not see a resolution. The view that sees only meaningless action motivated by forces ultimately unknown and inexplicable is the view that makes Hawthorne anticipate so much in the literature of the twentieth century.

Whether Dimmesdale or Hester was originally intended to be the main character is a fruitless question and perhaps not a pertinent one. Neither was so intended, probably. More than likely, the main lines of the *Scarlet Letter* were successfully maintained. The story was neither Hester's nor Dimmesdale's, but the story of both. Hawthorne uses themes familiar to him in showing a relatively weak and sensitive man and a very strong woman. The idea of Dimmesdale's willing death originates in Fanshawe's similar wish and resembles Young Goodman Brown's spiritual death. Hester is both one of the figures in the human drama and one of the enigmatic women in Hawthorne's work.

The story that results from Hawthorne's various ideas and intentions is a story of adultery, not in any sense one of love. Presumably a love attraction was in the background, but it derives from a mysterious force that the Greeks respected sufficiently to deify. Aphrodite, as she appears in Greek drama is, however, not a gentle or mischievous Cupid but the dread force that commanded Phaedra, Pasiphaë, and Medea. It was not the Puritan setting that caused events in the *Scarlet Letter*. The Puritan background was the best Hawthorne could do in finding a dark past for his new treatment of old themes, when the history of the new land, as he said, offered so little of the antique and the obscure. Events were caused by powerful unknown forces of the dark. The story is somehow timeless, yet not because adultery is everywhere a crime but because the conflict of such forces as are represented in the *Scarlet Letter* would be active anywhere. The suggestion is that a fundamental conflict occurs. No law is broken. As in *Hippolytus*, one fierce and impassive goddess has come into contact with another, and the problem must be worked out on the human level. The human actors themselves are innocent.

There is no redemption in the *Scarlet Letter* because as Hawthorne views the matter, there is no such thing as redemption. For that matter, there is no such thing as sin. But there are both suffering and condemnation. There is, too, a threat of extinction, which, however, does not occur. The need for irrational suffering apparently demands the continuation of life. The blackness is filled with the potential of threat and suffering.

This is the intuition that Hawthorne had to try to confine within a reasonable and believable framework of the historical novel and the historical setting. And he does exactly that. He persistently confines his own intuition. Where the *Scarlet Letter* is great, the intuition is uncontrolled in its essence, or it manages to express itself despite the limitations set by the artist.

Despite the references to Greek drama, the suggestion is not of Greek tragedy, except in its concern with elemental forces that present human beings with insoluble conflicts deriving from the unknown and irrational. Hawthorne may have been influenced by Greek tragedy and the Greek tragedy may offer a good many parallels, but there are many differences. There is no ritual, no hero, no culture threatened. The vision of hopelessness may be the same. The setting of the *Scarlet Letter* is Niflheim, and the time is myth. Hawthorne thus briefly illuminates a part of the underworld. Human life does not go there or derive from there. It exists there. Adultery is not a crime but human acts are the acts of sufferers. The question is not one of morality, except by chance and at times. The point is that life is condemned to existence. Existence itself is a part of the general condemnation. The whole of the world appears transcendentally meaningless.

IDENTITY AND KNOWLEDGE appear to be major themes also in the *House of the Seven Gables*. Numerous dualities occur in the language. On the one hand are secrecy and ignorance, on the other revelation and knowledge. The lengthy passage recording the conversation between Phoebe and Holgrave on the daguerreotype contains scores of references to various aspects of the general matter of knowledge and ignorance (III, 115–18). The problem of identity arises with regard to most of the main characters. The house itself, personified with its own face in the early chapters, is a mystery like its occupants. Identity is related further to both self-realization and location. Between the extremes is a complex of mysteries, perception of them ranging from unawareness to intuition. The progression is from secrecy through mystery to knowledge; from search for identity to recognition of place; and from innocence to experience. The problem is to arrive at knowledge in the midst of confusion and change. Human action itself for the most part reveals nothing.

The only possible source of truth apparently is intuition applied to the eyes and face, a method that Hawthorne uses often in this novel. Confrontations, such as are found in the *Scarlet Letter*, are even more deliberate in the *House of the Seven Gables*. Meetings occur between Phoebe and the Judge, Phoebe and Holgrave, Phoebe and Hepzibah, the Judge and Hepzibah, Hepzibah and

Clifford, and between Hepzibah and the portrait of Colonel Pyncheon. The daguerreotype process emphasizes the
seeing, substituting pictures for direct confrontations, ena-
bling Holgrave to confront both Clifford and the Judge
and attempt to discern their characters.

A great many references can be found to the eyes.
"Phoebe's eyes sank" under the Judge's look (III, 146).
The artist has "deep, thoughtful, all-observant eyes" (III,
189). Hepzibah looks into Clifford's face. Holgrave is "too
calm and cool an observer. Phoebe felt his eye, often . . ."
(III, 213). The young Italian has a "quick professional
eye" (III, 196). The girls talked "about what they called
the witchcraft of Maule's eye" (III, 227). The power of
the eye is central to the episode between Alice and Matthew Maule. He commands Alice: " 'fix your eyes on
mine!' " (III, 242). And he commands Gervayse: " 'Be-
hold your daughter!' " (III, 244). The wizard eye, characteristic of the Maules, effective still in Holgrave, is what
allows him to fix his eyes on Phoebe with so much power.

The staring eyes of the Judge are pointed out on numerous occasions, including that on which a fly crawls toward
one of them on the morning after his death. A "gimlet-
eyed old gentleman," seeing Clifford and Hepzibah on the
train, is "curious to make them out" (III, 307). Ned has
the wide eyes of a child, and even the chickens throw side
glances at Phoebe with an aristocratic mixture of curiosity
and reserve. Hepzibah's near-sight is the basis of an epithet. Clifford's eyes are sensitive and may have roved once,
as the Judge's did. Many of the references are in no way
unusual of course. But underneath all this is the problem
of seeing; and, in addition, the power of vision to determine, influence, and know; to perceive character with
certainty.

The face of each of the Pyncheons is described.
Hepzibah is a "dark-arrayed, pale-faced, lady-like old
figure . . ." (III, 54). Judge Pyncheon's face conceals hypocrisy. Clifford's face is transformed. Uncle Venner's, "so
familiar to the town" (III, 189-90), is daguerreotyped.
The face of the greedy and acquisitive monkey recalls that

of Judge Pyncheon; just as its Highland bonnet, like the hens's crests, recalls Hepzibah's turban. Clifford sees a face in Maule's Well, and he cannot bear to look at Hepzibah's face.

But observation is not assurance, particularly when observation may have been distorted or inaccurate. This is the case with the public eye which observes in "uneducated entanglement and confusion" (III, 95). The public is continuously deceived throughout the action. The only relief in this deception—public self-deception, really—is that where so many rumors exist, one or two may by chance be true.

The public does know immediately of Clifford's arrival, knowledge that is a compliment only to its propensity for ill-natured prying. The public is otherwise characterized by rumor, misapprehension, poor observation, mistaken judgment, injustice, and hypocrisy. And if Dixey's prognostications (III, 344) are characteristic, they make even the Yankee's business ability doubtful.

The first important mistake is the conviction of Maule as a wizard, a delusion shared by the public leaders. The second lies in the character of Colonel Pyncheon, whom Higginson's funeral sermon extols, as the newspaper later does the Judge, for his public service and his virtues. The public is wrong as to the whereabouts of Clifford and Hepzibah and even fails, with one exception, to note their walk to the station. Public knowledge generally is derived from the "chimney-corner tradition," a means by which superstition passes for truth. Despite some gossip about both Colonel and Judge, the public, led by church and press, join in helping them to maintain their hypocritical stations. And Dixey's misapprehensions lead him to an elaborate misconstruction of all the facts of the Judge's death, a situation emphasized by the imagination of the children who appear to represent the public when the Judge's death is suspected. But, says the narrator, the "common observer" would "understand nothing of the case" (III, 348). Judge Pyncheon and the consenting world so well cooperate that he is estimated to be precisely all that he seems. The Maules, on the other hand, have been misunderstood from the beginning: the first inhabitant, son, and grandson. First, they were thought to be wizards. Afterwards, before the episode with Matthew and Alice, they had been supposed to "harbor no resentment."

The deception is thorough. There are three major supposed crimes: Maule's sorcery, the Colonel's murder, and the bachelor's murder. Both the Colonel and the bachelor uncle, like the Judge, seem to die naturally. Everything else is only a rumor, or illusion, except the rôle of the Judge; and that is known only to a mesmerist whom Holgrave has ferreted out. Almost nothing is really known.

There are numerous apertures in the house, ways of communicating, but communication usually is distorted and observation is inexact. Curtains, draperies, and the elm keep the interior shadowy. The shop entrance is, significantly perhaps, a half door, its glass half being curtained over, to Phoebe's surprise, on the morning of her return. Glimpses from the outside only give rise to rumor, when, for example, Alice is seen or when the "sable face of a slave" (III, 228) appears for an instant. Uncomprehended activity goes on within. The shop door yields grudgingly throughout, and on the morning after the Judge's death it admits none. Nor does peering within reveal anything except another door, closed to Ned's eyes and open to the butcher's, who, however, mistakes death for life. The arched window, the main source of contact between the house and the public, reveals to Clifford not the real world but a parade and a puppet show. And to the public it gives a mistaken impression of Clifford's sanity. All the secrecy of the house is emphasized by Phoebe's repeated symbolic exclamation: " 'throw open the doors!' " (III, 361) to the public to reveal the Judge's death. The spell is finally broken when Hepzibah and Clifford return and the door is opened.

The parchment, having to do with the dichotomy between reality and imagination, represents only a fancied property. The chart of the property, the long-possessed symbol of the claim to location and stature, is one of the "ornamental articles of furniture" (III, 49). Significantly, it is "not engraved, but the handiwork of some skilful old draughtsman, and grotesquely illuminated with pictures of Indians and wild beasts, among which was seen a lion; the natural history of the region being as little known as its geography, which was put down most fantastically awry" (III, 49–50). Where, in short, is the Pyncheon claim to property, if representation is thus fanciful and distorted?

The portrait of the Colonel, one gathers, in fact represents reality, at least to the extent that the verbal and conceptual paradox allows. Hepzibah's confrontation with the portrait early in the action introduces a motif that carries throughout the story. With scowl, Bible, and staff it will defend its unwelcome secret of the vault until the Maulean magic reveals what not even the spectral Pyncheons or the mesmerized Alice could reveal, though apparently Maule's grandson did know of the whereabouts, since the secret is a part of the family tradition.

And the painter had caught the essence of the character of Clifford in the miniature. The Colonel's "indirect character . . . seemed to be brought out in a kind of spiritual relief" in the portrait, for "the painter's deep conception of his subject's inward traits has wrought itself into the essence of the picture, and is seen after the superficial coloring has been rubbed off by time" (III, 79).

Hawthorne was particularly interested in the symbolism of the daguerreotype, which magically used sunshine to reveal character beneath the composed features presented to the world; and of course Holgrave, in the main line of the Maulean wizards, is the one to discover the ugliness that Judge Pyncheon conceals from the world. He has the artificial eye for it, the daguerreotype, and the aid of both "heaven's eye" and his own exceptionally perceptive mesmeric ability. Thus, the reflective surface of his miniature reveals what the mirror does not, successfully, it seems. For Phoebe's suggestion that daguerreotypes are more apt to distort than reveal is based on ignorance. She has seen only the portrait of the Colonel, and not the Judge, who is the subject of Holgrave's miniature. Then, too, she has

already admitted the artistic power to perceive, in des-
crying Clifford's nature from looking at Hepzibah's miniature of his youth.

Various other states of observation and perception appear. Phoebe's innocence often is puzzled or startled. She
is bewildered in sensing the presence of Clifford on the
night of his arrival. But over against this deficiency is her
intuitive perception. Yet, throughout, until the resolution,
Phoebe lacks knowledge of facts and identities, symbolic
of course of her innocence.

Hepzibah's affliction with near-sight is intentionally
symbolic both of her limited perceptive capacity and of an
unintentional impression she gives of being one of the
scowling Pyncheons of the main line. The lengthy passage
dealing with her thoughts, as she goes for Clifford while
the Judge waits, is a dissertation on states of perception.
But she at once recognizes Phoebe's genuineness and feebly
intuits that of Holgrave, though puzzled by him.

The Judge's perceptive ability lies in the business way,
and a good deal is made of the paradox between his native
sagacity and his delusion about hidden riches of which he
insists that Clifford has knowledge. This delusion of
course Clifford shares, and it proceeds from a paradox:
Clifford's real, but fancifully represented, knowledge of a
real key to riches, the map, which exists, but which is no
longer of value. Thus, actually, the Judge is right about
the key to wealth in so far as Clifford has properly represented his own knowledge of it. Clifford, too, has his
schemes, and Hepzibah has a remarkable flight of imagination early in the action, in dreaming of a rich position
and an Oriental turban, the latter the symbol of a queen,
presumably.

Holgrave has knowledge that will aid Clifford and
Hepzibah, as well as the Judge, in seeing, but claims, at
least, not to know how he can use it for the benefit of the
innocent. He, in short, has much of the knowledge that
Phoebe lacks, throughout, and some of that lacked by all
the others. Yet, he has not the knowledge to fathom what
is to occur, despite his feeling that something will.

Both the observer and the artist are represented by Holgrave, who will not anticipate in the drama and whose conversion to a participant's rôle is in part the story of his identity. His refusal to exercise his mesmeric powers over Phoebe, along with his loss of the quality of cold, impartial observation, aids in removal of the curse. What happens, more than likely, is that he refrains from committing Matthew's probable crime of physical seduction. The curse is removed because the crimes are ceased. Holgrave instead resigns himself to the anonymity that Hawthorne designed for Edward Walcott.

The problem of identity is one of simple recognition of names and faces as well as of character. On Phoebe's emergence from the cab, Hepzibah at first says: " 'Who can it be?' " (III, 90) and then concludes it to be her cousin. There is rarely hesitation about Phoebe. Holgrave recognizes her at once. When she is introduced to Clifford, he recognizes her, despite his mental weakness. The Judge is only momentarily under a misapprehension, then recognizes Phoebe by the resemblance to her father. Everyone can tell Phoebe something about herself. And both Clifford and the Judge call her "near name."

Phoebe at once recognizes Clifford by his resemblance to the miniature, imprint of identity, and by the faded robe he wears. The clothing and the half-knowledge cause her, however, to mistake the Judge's miniature for a representation of the countenance in the Colonel's portrait. But she at once recognizes the Judge, when he appears in the shop, by his resemblance to both the portrait and the miniature.

Hepzibah's relative lack of identity is emphasized by the fact of her holding the property only during her lifetime and by the fact that she is not so much of the main line or of society as even to receive her mail to announce Phoebe's arrival. But too of course there is hope, and her dreams of riches are dreams of position and identity—recognition among her kin.

The miniature of Clifford that introduces him is in ironic contrast to the view of him given in the narrative present. In the miniature he is the beautiful and sensitive artist, Oberon, the perfect youth. When he returns from prison he must continue to face not only his lost time but also must, it seems, either die or to some extent regain his mental loss. The ambiguous state he is in urges some kind of change. In a sense he is a Doppelgänger. He observes his other, like Wakefield, in reverse and observes himself dead. He has not only skipped a long period of life and experience; he has actually regressed to childhood. Clifford's, then, is a peculiar case of search for identity, not confined to search for a place in society. With the return of his senses, he must not only regain the sensitivity of youth but also adjust to having passed blindly over that period into age. Frequent references are made to Clifford's weak mind. The narrator finds him imbecile, or "partly imbecile" (III, 190). The episode with a knife grinder refers facetiously to Clifford's dull wits—it is an author too self-conscious who writes the scene. He prefers the slow-paced, old-fashioned vehicles, and there seems little doubt that the preference is meant further to suggest his slow, dull thinking; just as the fast train ride is associated with his sudden mental vigor.

Clifford's whole problem, then, is to become himself again, with proper allowances for age. And what is the process of identity when it involves insanity, when it is not the normal mind that seeks place? Besides, of course he is only released, not exonerated; though the narrator will add a note in the resolution to the effect that Clifford did not think it worth while to have himself cleared. Clifford has a double job of adjustment, a double search to make. And despite Hepzibah's significant assurances, he does not feel at home. The insanity is in some measure compensated, however, by a certain kind of sharpened perception.

The problem of identity appears though to be specifically Holgrave's. Dependent in part on self-realization, it must be established in all respects. Not even the courthouse records list his name. Hawthorne uses the metaphor of the change of garb symbolically with him too, in that he has assumed many rôles. Yet, says the narrator, Holgrave has kept his identity. That is, with all his wandering among the lower classes, his conscience is clear and his character upright. He has only responded to his dissatisfaction, or, in short, he has wandered a journey in search of himself, of his rôle and place, a reflection of autobiography. His proper rôle is not that of individualist and reformer of the *status quo*. He at least feels that his real identity lies in casting off the mask as individualist and observer and becoming a social animal. He wants to let himself be absorbed, to be nameless and anonymous, like Coverdale, Kenyon, and Walcott.

It is quite as though Hawthorne propounded the Hegelian dialectic. A thing, a person, contains its opposite. A person is not what he is. For the subject of identity, this may mean development and change in a character, and such occurs to Holgrave in the course of the novel, though predicted and though abrupt and unconvincing. That is, Hawthorne tells us, as he did with Hester, that a change has occurred. But the problem of identity is difficult for both the individual and for those acquaintances who seek to know him. There are flux and change to take account of. And what a person really is may depend on the machinations of chance; what he seems to be may have to be perceived through a good deal of apparent hypocrisy.

Hypocrisy makes it difficult to determine Judge Pyncheon's character, and with him the context broadens considerably because he has a good deal of renown. Hawthorne spends more than a page on the "splendid rubbish" (iii, 274) of the Judge's public life. It is the public that he deceives. Morally, the Judge is not what he seems, but his problem is more complex than that. He lacks two things in being whole, ironic as it may be. He needs to be put in place as the perpetrator of any crime that was committed, and he needs to come into his ancestral position fully, as owner of the property in Maine.

An ironic commentary on the Judge's identity appears in the vigil scene in the account of the activities that will not be performed. The newspaper thrown on Hepzibah's doorstep conceals the Judge's card, on which is the record of his proposed itinerary of the preceding day; the paper will have been published for once without any account of the Judge's activities, and without even a notice of his death. The day's news will in fact cover the last symbolic remnant of the Judge's identity and of his position, and it will make his death insignificant in the current of social and political events. The Judge's death will be old news before it is officially recorded. And the newspaper will of course record selection of another candidate for the governor's chair, while Judge Pyncheon sits wide-eyed in the ancestral chair, his life ignored as well as his death. Thus much is valued his position and his aspiration to the high position of state office. The Judge is put out of society by its ignorance of his whereabouts. He changes place with Clifford who will replace him in the account of the following day. And of course the paper cannot say that Judge Pyncheon has erected a new stone to mark the grave, the identity, of his "beloved" wife. It must also be significant for the Judge's stature that while "he would have made a good and massive portrait" (III, 77), there exists of him only a miniature. It means perhaps that the Judge knows himself, as Chillingworth came to, but Hawthorne does not show what he thinks, except in dialogue and action.

The theme of property joins those of social position and hypocrisy. The Pyncheons have possessed an artificial identity in being respected hypocrites and scoundrels. Yet, they have never acquired the appurtenances of their own estimates of their position. The symbol of the position lies hidden in the vault, and is represented only by the ornamental chart; their identity is, in short, undermined, stolen away, by the wizardry of the Maules. This whole matter is represented in the episode between Matthew and Alice, wherein Alice loses her individuality to Matthew.

Even the identity of the minor character, Uncle Venner, is discussed. He is a "miscellaneous old gentleman, partly himself, but, in good measure, somebody else; patched together, too, of different epochs; an epitome of times and fashions" (III, 82–83). Hawthorne has grouped a number of innocents and half-wits to set off against the sagacious Pyncheons and industrious Yankees. But he attributes a good deal of wisdom to Uncle Venner, who counsels Hepzibah sagely on operating her shop. On the last page he is "wise Uncle Venner," left musing on his new epithet because " 'folks used to set me down among the simple ones, in my younger days!' " (III, 376) when he had been "regarded as rather deficient, than otherwise, in his wits" (III, 82). Yet, he fills a "place which would else have been vacant in the apparently crowded world" (III, 81). That he exists, in short, appears right. Compare this comment, however, with the commentary on death, Judge Pyncheon's in particular; usually "the individual is present among us, mixed up with the daily revolution of affairs, and affording a definite point for observation. At his decease, there is only a vacancy, and a momentary eddy . . ." (III, 366). The individual is not particularly important.

The *House of the Seven Gables* is Hawthorne's most nearly mature work, but in it he unfortunately attempts to be constructive and to avoid an unhappy ending. He may also have been too much under the influence of mundane, autobiographical considerations. He collects a group of persons who are merely unpleasant. They do not have the stature of villains, nor the strength to maintain the curse on the house. Such affection as Hawthorne may have shows only in the handling of the figure of Hepzibah. In general, he is either indifferent or indulgent. The heinousness of Judge Pyncheon's crime is but suggested, and his punishment is nothing more than a set piece in which the author rejoices. Hawthorne does seem to concentrate on the figures, trying to determine what motivates them. But he studies character and motivation, not these individuals. Individually, they are of no more importance to Hawthorne than to Holgrave. If they were, he would give them strength.

In so far as the Pyncheons are individuals, they have long been enervated by luxury. Hawthorne's occasional references to the characters of the Judge and Clifford indicate that he wished to suggest that the curse was maintained in part by the lustful nature of the Pyncheons, not merely by their acquisitiveness. They were a family of Sybarites, to use Hawthorne's term. Hepzibah's dreams suggest that she too was a Sybarite, though not of the main line of the Pyncheons. This characteristic makes it easy for the Judge to tyrannize over Hepzibah and Clifford, but the suggestion is that both the Judge and his son too are enervated by their indulgences. Phoebe of course, associated with the yeoman of the country, is uncontaminated. But when she and Holgrave have become accustomed to their wealth, will they not also become degenerate through luxury?

Consideration of the *House of the Seven Gables* as a whole, and as the most mature if not the most appealing of Hawthorne's works, provides an opportunity for discussing some of the doctrines usually attributed to Hawthorne. The warmth of the public heart, for example, as suggested above, is nonexistent. The public, in this work, as in other major works of Hawthorne, is unpleasant, ignorant, and antagonistic. It is true that Hawthorne remarks of Dimmesdale's last sermon that it is an appeal to the "great heart of mankind." The observation suggests a tentative sympathy, which, however, may reflect the feelings of Dimmesdale rather than those of Hawthorne. If the sentiment is Hawthorne's the reference may be to the collective heart. Or, indeed, the reference may be quite intended, within the context, as a genuine conviction of the basic kindness of human nature. Hawthorne may have had such a conviction occasionally. But no more is required, surely, than the opening scene of the *Scarlet Letter* to indicate how Hawthorne *portrays* the public. The portrayal of the *House of the Seven Gables* is less severe, but that of "The Gentle Boy" is much more so. The matter is hardly alleviated by a suggestion that the severity reflects only on Puritans of an earlier age. "The Gray Champion" presents a somewhat more pleasant view of the public, but this and other stories, such as "Edward Randolph's Portrait," present the public rather as the collective spirit of an injured nation. Public feelings otherwise are hardly considered, in these tales. On the other hand, "Dr. Higginbotham's Catastrophe" shows but a gullible public that is as charmed by rumor as that of the *House of the Seven Gables* is. The early pages of the *English Notebooks* indicate that Hawthorne was disturbed by the shabby crowds in Liverpool. "The Great Stone Face" shows the public to be fickle and naïve at best. Theoretically, perhaps, Hawthorne had a consideration for the public, but he does not often reveal a conviction that people are warmhearted.

The theme of the new Adam is hardly tenable as an explanation of the *House of the Seven Gables*. Hawthorne expects nothing from a new Adam. He is too much impressed by the feeling that a new world, humanity being such as "Earth's Holocaust" suggests, would only grow like the old. There is nothing to be done. Reform is of no use. Even as Hawthorne writes the *House of the Seven Gables*, he creates, in Coverdale, a character who vows that he would not cross the street to aid a cause. The happy ending to some extent derives from the action of the book, but the end has come. There is no future for Holgrave and Phoebe. They have gone to anonymity.

There is little constructive talk of home. Phoebe, the character with whom the doctrine of the hearth should be associated, leaves home and comes to play the rôle of the maiden who makes men ordinary. Clifford and Hepzibah hardly have a home. Clifford explicitly rejects the hearth, in his conversation on the train. And Holgrave says that the family should be lost in the "great, obscure mass of humanity" (III, 222).

The doctrine of violation may now be discussed somewhat explicitly. If Hawthorne's concept of violation of the human heart is divested of the machinery of such stories as "The Birthmark," it closely resembles what occurs in the fall in *Paradise Lost* and in Goodman Brown's experience. Being is laid bare. A man's personal secrets become known, and he gets the knowledge that others share his shortcomings as a human being. Violation, as Hawthorne uses the concept, is psychological, having little to do with sin or theology. It is a fiendish crime against human being, an obvious traduction of individuality, or a rape of the mind. The idea could be put into a theological framework, but this is dubiously Hawthorne's intention. Hawthorne was particularly aware of violation because he did, as he said, see into the hearts of people. He may also have had some unfortunate personal experiences. Coverdale goes to some length to avoid being controlled by Hollingsworth. Hawthorne must often have felt enough knowledge and power to control others, and perhaps he even at times had the inclination to use it. Thus, he in effect drops Milton's theological framework and his assumptions, retaining only enough of the conventional terminology to give his ideas a context. He needs a language, and psychology had not yet provided a vocabulary.

"Some man of powerful character," a notebook entry reads, "to command a person, morally subjected to him, to perform some act. The commanding person to suddenly die; and, for all the rest of his life, the subjected one continues to perform the act" (92). Hawthorne used some version of this idea to plot everything he wrote after, and including, "Rappaccini's Daughter." Thus, perhaps one makes fate appear immanent. Chillingworth, Westervelt and Old Moodie, Matthew Maule, the Spectre of the Catacombs, and Dr. Grimshawe all are such figures as the quotation proposes. So is Holgrave, though he is not malicious. The violation is interaction among the characters in which some malevolent incarnation of the wily servant, perhaps based on the figure of Iago though not of his stature, operative but often personally insignificant, formulates an unpleasant outcome. In the *House of the Seven Gables*, except for the remark in regard to Holgrave's abstinence from using his powers, Hawthorne only plots the action. People are violated surely, but showing opposition to it is not the conscious doctrine, though the results are shown. Hawthorne shows the violation that occurs all the time in human relationships. He sets up figures to represent fate and the unknown, the limitations on being. But in rejecting the symbolic figures, Hawthorne also rejects the whole set of conditions that in making man what he is also made him limited beyond improvement. The creator prevents humanity from ever being what man aspires to be.

Hawthorne may have had the *Oresteia* in mind when he wrote the *House of the Seven Gables.* This work offered a precedent for exonerating the last male of the line and for closing off the past. Yet, in the *House of the Seven Gables,* very little is established by removal of the curse, and no very impressive examination of the relationship between past and present occurs. Actually, Hawthorne has neglected the dramatic potential of these themes, if his intention was to analyze them. It seems, rather, as if he concentrated quite on the present. What he really does is to urge everyone to fit into the great flowing stream of the present, which constantly becomes the past. He would like everything and everyone neatly placed and neatly passed on. There is little desire for something new to replace the passing. The Pyncheon name will be lost with Clifford's death, and the Pyncheon house has already passed into other hands. The approach is negative. Things are asked to go away or to let themselves be put away. The desire is for nothing *but* the past, and in this sense the past is nothing. The view is nihilistic, yet passively so, for Hawthorne does not enjoin so much action and energy as would be needed for destruction. There is no emphasis upon a future or even upon a meaningful present. Hawthorne says that Holgrave was mistaken to think that he could change the world or to think that the world would change, except by a slow natural process (III, 216). That may or may not be an expression of faith. A year later, Coverdale does not claim anything. Holgrave makes it clear that he is indifferent.

Critical theorizing on such matters as love and goodness can hardly alleviate the harshness of the situation in the *House of the Seven Gables,* despite such support as may be provided by the contrived action found there. Try as he may, Hawthorne does not make one feel any hope. There is only temporary cessation of conflict.

AS IN THE OTHER novels, the mystery of the *Blithedale Romance* centers on sexual incidents of one kind or another, and both the sexual mystery and the question of identity deal with whether Zenobia is a woman who has known love and what effect the experience may have had on her character. The *Scarlet Letter* dealt with the scrutiny of Hester; the *Blithedale Romance* deals with a more suggestive and covert scrutiny of Zenobia. And though Coverdale writes an apologetic on his examination of Hollingsworth, he unabashedly dissects Zenobia, only to leave the mystery unsolved. Zenobia's character remains enigmatic except for Coverdale's feeling that she ought to have been an actress, an observation that deepens the mystery about her and suggests the bigger problem of what a woman is.

The problem of knowledge is emphasized by the ignorance of the mesmerist, the one who should know but whose knowledge is limited, whatever he may know of Zenobia. Though a disguised barebones, the clothing and the false teeth, as the rumor, being symbolic of the man, he is himself an enigma. His hypnotic powers fail with Priscilla at the last; and he is one of the few quite neglected characters in Hawthorne's work, as if he were only an instrument used to devise mystery.

A good deal more is made of clothing in the *Blithedale Romance* than in the *House of the Seven Gables,* the most obvious use being of course Priscilla's veil. Zenobia's use of a veil in her legend suggests the idea of one person's control over another's individuality. The clothing symbolism extends so far as to the use of smocks by the colonists, a habit that causes Coverdale to be taken as a churl by Westervelt, in a scene in which Coverdale acts like one.

Old Moodie uses clothing disguise both by choice and by necessity. The patch over his eye is both a disguise and a symbol of his dim wits. The symbolism here extends so far as to refer in some detail to the clothing he wore in former days. The general mystery and Moodie's duplicity are evident not only from his double life but also from his half-concealment and yet sly knowledge of what occurs. He is in fact the one who knows most, except Westervelt, and he thus is an interesting foil for the clever mesmerist, who gets some of his knowledge illegitimately.

Old Moodie's patch is a symbol of concealment that disguises identity and suggests the whole of the mystery concerning the origins of the family, a mystery that lies beneath the current action even when it does not account for the action. Hawthorne obviously did not consider Moodie important enough to show more of him in the plot. But, too, he likes showing the subtle influence of Moodie's past act. He wishes to keep the source hidden as nearly as possible, and he must have controlled with some effort the urge to present a scene in which Moodie removes the patch and reveals himself as the heir to Zenobia's fortune. But it is an indication of Hawthorne's wish to show the influence and results of Moodie's action without showing him in action that Zenobia's fortune is allowed to devolve upon Priscilla by Moodie's agency, without the appearance of Moodie himself. Moodie's last remarks at parting with Zenobia and her revelation of the loss of the fortune, which Hawthorne emphasizes by repetition, are sufficient to show what occurred as a result of her betrayal of Priscilla. Even Westervelt's influence, though different from Moodie's and forming a second theme for the book, derives from the secrecy of Moodie's actions subsequent to the original crime.

Disguise pervades the book, beginning with the veiled

lady and continuing with Zenobia's sheet and the masquerade in the forest. As usual, in Hawthorne, the action rises to a point where someone much concerned stops, is placed in the forefront, and made to ask someone for his identity. In Zenobia's fable, Theodore says, " 'Mysterious creature . . . I would know who and what you are!' " (III, 112).

The variety of the disguise and identity theme is increased by the suggestion that these descendants of the Puritans who had detached themselves for the purpose of beginning a new community in a new world are repeating that process, with similar purpose. The irony of such an intention is emphasized by the fact that not only will Hollingsworth the reformer commit a crime against the community in taking their property but also his purpose is reformation of criminals in that colony which the first Puritans set up as a crimeless haven for saints.

Hollingsworth is perhaps better known than any of the others, on the surface. But his true character, if Coverdale properly assesses it, is not known by Zenobia and Priscilla. We have the testimony of the clothing at least that he is so genuine as only to change the smith's garb for the colony smock. But why is he so bent on reforming criminals?

Nothing is sure in the *Blithedale Romance,* and if Coverdale needs justification for prying, he ought to be excused on the argument of survival in a world where nothing is sure. He is surrounded by disguise and deceit and by passions strong enough to commit numerous crimes. The reformer of criminals works here among unknown criminals who associate with him everyday. Here is Hawthorne's comment on humanity and character. Priscilla and Coverdale are the only exceptions, and indeed Coverdale may possibly have had his own innocent fling at the veiled lady as Theodore of whom Zenobia speaks. Then his love and his hints of knowledge would be explained.

When Moodie first meets Coverdale, he says, " 'I wonder, sir, . . . whether you know a lady whom they call

Zenobia?'" The following paragraph reveals that she wears in the name "'a sort of mask in which she comes before the world, retaining all the privileges of privacy—a contrivance, in short, like the white drapery of the Veiled Lady, only a little more transparent'" (III, 8). Westervelt later says that he is willing to know Zenobia by any "cognomen" (III, 93). Coverdale's analogy has now placed all three of the family before him. The action can begin on the main problem of determining who and what Zenobia is.

When Coverdale meets Zenobia, the mystery leads only to more questions, with a good deal of speculation and with an apparent intuition that gradually suggests answers to queries about her past. The original question of who Zenobia is will be in some measure complicated by the variant that asks what she is. For though Coverdale finally is able to provide a good deal of information, it is in great part information that he did not seek and did not know to seek. And though he has suspected the passion of her nature, he has not known the extent of it. Intuition has provided him with the truth only after the fact. The question is left as to what she was, particularly in Coverdale's self-query as to whether she really intended to drown herself, or whether she would have drowned herself if she had known how death would make her look.

Furthermore, despite all the reader learns, the questions presented at the meeting with Moodie are not answered. One presumes that Zenobia was Fauntelroy's daughter, but one does not know if this is the name she conceals in using Zenobia or if she conceals her uncle's, or if her passionate nature, which now makes her appear to Coverdale to be fully a woman, has caused her to change it to some other at some time in the past.

Yet, though Zenobia's self-confidence suggests that she is aware of her own mystery and has assurance in it, there is much that she does not know of matters very close to her. In fact, what she does not know amounts to considerably more than she knows. She does not know of her father, of her sister, or of their relationship with a third person, Westervelt, whose artifices give him information and influence, though he, for his part, may not have known of the relationship of the family.

On another level, Zenobia has greater importance as one of Hawthorne's enigmatic representatives of the eternal feminine. Hawthorne stares fixedly at the secrets of Hester, Zenobia, and Miriam. Hester stood before all eyes on the scaffold; the curiosity about Miriam's secrets is discussed below. The scene presenting the rescue of Zenobia's body is almost fantastically suggestive. The dead body is still Zenobia, now on display before all the men who have wondered about her secrets. If the wound made by Hollingsworth with the grapple is not doubly symbolic, Silas Foster's attempt to extend her distorted body symbolizes the whole masculine effort to dominate her. The incident, despite its origins in a real incident, would be remarkable artistry if the age were not so delicate as to make it vulgar. Perhaps, however, it is artistry, since Hawthorne wrote the scene with disregard for the delicacy.

Zenobia here is queen of women, and the men violate her in every respect. She has lost in all attempts to retain her individuality and her mysteries. Emotionally and physically, she is violated. She represents the whole vast secret that men find in the other sex that makes women both attractive and repulsive. Yet, the inflexibility of her corpse is like her inflexible refusal to be dominated or to be usual. And she is finally sent off to the women as their queen, all her intimacies revealed, though the enigma of her being will remain unknown.

Priscilla and her father have the information that others lack, though they presumably do not know of Zenobia's relationship to Westervelt. And though Moodie knows Hollingsworth, none of them knows what chance influence Hollingsworth will have on the fortunes of the family. In short, only the apparently insignificant in this story have knowledge, and though it is not such as to make them significant, it makes them cooperative and leads to their survival. Zenobia, who apparently knows most of herself, knows little. And the chorus who does know most, has to stand ineffectively by and let the action proceed to its dénouement.

There is then the secondary matter of the great amount of observation that results from the fact of so much mystery. Zenobia is not only above it, but her fate is to be victimized and to be informed only when it is too late to act. Westervelt is one of that type in Hawthorne who simply has knowledge without any explanation given as to how he acquired it, like Chillingworth whom he resembles as much in the rôle he plays as in character. Hollingsworth, significantly, is quite blind to perception or observation. Coverdale, Moodie, Priscilla, Westervelt, and Zenobia, all, however, do a good deal of observation of one another. Westervelt takes Coverdale by surprise, in the forest, then Coverdale spies on him and Zenobia from the tree.

Emphasis is on seeing and observing, on solving the mysteries that form the basis of the plot, on penetration of disguises and finding out who people are, on establishing identities. On the other hand, the attempt is made to conceal identities. Zenobia, with apparently the most secrets, is, despite her strength of character, sensitive to Coverdale's observation because it threatens her identity. She refuses to be too well-known, both physically and emotionally. These characters are not intimate with one another; they have secrets and do not know one another. Zenobia more than many a Hawthorne character strives for individuality, against both her creator and her associates. It is fundamental that her passionate nature is not allowed to identify with a lover and her being consequently not allowed to be fulfilled. And it is significant for the subject of identity that discovery of who Priscilla is leads nowhere in particular. For once she recovers being from Westervelt, not of her own, she subjugates to Hollingsworth, identifying with him and sacrificing herself to her love. In short, Priscilla's identity is persistently violated and is in the first place dependent on another for completion, perhaps as a way of showing Zenobia what she must do. Yet, Priscilla's symbolic veil and purses attract men to a kind of net that is like that of Ellen, Phoebe, and Hilda. She makes men ordinary.

Coverdale's actions may follow on his taking the advice of Septimius' manuscript: "Do not any foolish good act" (XI, 341). Hawthorne would have got the lesson from Don Quixote's good acts and perhaps from a severe interpretation of the Nicomachean ethics. Coverdale offers sympathy without passion, just as the chorus does and just as he says he does. He simply makes too much of the point. And of course he contrasts with those who have passions, as Kenyon and Holgrave do. Though Coverdale protests his individuality, he survives because he stays out of the action; he does not appear individualistic, but only unravished.

Coverdale chooses not to get involved with anyone, neither Hollingsworth, Moodie, Zenobia—nor Kossuth. And though he makes an attempt to prevent Westervelt from taking Priscilla, he does not rescue her as Hollingsworth eventually does. The incident shows the ineffectiveness of the outsider, points up the sin of the others, and perhaps indicates that Coverdale ought to have involved himself more. But Hawthorne objected to reformers—"humours"—who are identified with causes and thus distort their own beings. A belief, in its simplest effect and its greatest, is a limitation of what one is or can become; it is a sin against the Hegelian dialectic.

Coverdale is akin to Fanshawe and Septimius, younger brothers of Holgrave and Kenyon, if older in conception. These younger ones are somehow black sheep in the family. They refuse to become subject to the eternal feminine or to society, choosing instead a different kind of anonymity. Coverdale moves in and out of place, maintaining what he calls his individuality and remaining detached. He must be the most enigmatic figure in Hawthorne's work, but not because he deserves so much attention, as a character.

Coverdale at first has place, bachelor rooms in town. Joining the Blithedale experiment is for him a step out of society and place. Here is an ironic search for place in isolation from society. Coverdale's anomalous position is one coming between, though after, Hawthorne's intuitive solution of Fanshawe's problem of life and his mature handling of the theme in the *House of the Seven Gables*, where marriage provides the means by which Holgrave adjusts to life, though he is a somewhat less frenzied character.

All Blithedale is search for place, and Coverdale epitomizes the search and epitomizes the failure to find the goal. He returns from the society of Blithedale, which is a group outside society, to a hotel room where, his apartment gone, he isolates himself, only hearing and watching life without being in it. His new foray out into life, his one action, amounts to nothing. He is inconsequent in the rôle he takes upon himself. A foolish good act amounts to nothing, and so perhaps does all good action, and all action, except for the evil that may derive from dubious ideals.

Still, perhaps Coverdale's chief problem is the one to which he so often refers, the attempt to keep his own identity, such as and whatever it is. This causes him to refuse to join Hollingsworth, in a scene in which he must strive to utter his single everlasting nay, an answer evoked by his unconscious, that enables him to escape possible violation from Hollingsworth. Coverdale is so much affected that he would choose to make no reply or to talk at length without decision, but if he must reply, his reason is of no use. Only his unconscious life wish, as it were, avails, and he must say "No" from the depths. The monosyllable saves him. Still, Coverdale's much talk of identity sounds as if it reflected Hawthorne's thinking about specific experiences at Brook Farm. It does not necessarily fit what Hawthorne has to say about nonentity and anonymity. Yet, Coverdale resembles Kenyon and Holgrave in striving to avoid the dominant passions in general and specifically in their threat to his identity and his being. Zenobia would be as dominant as Hollingsworth. Priscilla, whom he does not really seek, would complement his own nature perhaps, but Hawthorne chooses to let him go unattached. Coverdale has got somehow to represent a major crisis in Hawthorne's life.

Hawthorne must have realized intuitively at the start of his career that the way of the world was not to be much improved by schemes for change or improvement. Perhaps the feeling for the static was influenced by eighteenth-century thought sufficiently that he did not really want much change. A sensitive person who becomes very thoughtful only finds himself depressed by all the changes needed, and he becomes a repository for complaints about the ills. Not only can he do very little at his utmost, but also whatever he might do helps very little and for but a short time. Pride would keep some men from becoming so seriously absorbed in a reform as to be the source of jokes. Serious involvement would detract from a man's whole-ness. Besides, one soon tires of offering sympathy. He is soon too emotionally tired to have any resources of sympathy left to offer.

Coverdale shows all this, and his character represents Hawthorne's ambivalent feelings about individuality, effort, society, and place. When there is so much to do in order to make improvements, one can only watch the hand of fate with a fascinated and helpless interest. To keep sane, he develops a cold detachment and may even smile from what he thinks is a deeper wisdom. It all means that Hawthorne's sensitivity forced him to defend himself from involvement, no matter how much he wished to involve. And if he could not practice his own preachments, it is no more than is true of all other cod-ifiers of ideal codes.

One cannot know if Hawthorne means to show in Coverdale what happens when one refuses to get in-volved—the consequent loneliness—or if he urges against involvement. But it is probably both, a portrayal of the situation, a character who would like to be involved and who cannot force himself to be. Hawthorne's own unset-tled doctrine is probably reflected here. Only the year before in the *House of the Seven Gables* he has in Holgrave a character who does join society and lose individuality, and in the *Marble Faun* two couples lose themselves. Kenyon and Hilda are the new Adam and Eve, though nothing is expected of them, while Miriam and Donatello are the old Adam and Eve expelled from Eden.

The *Marble Faun* is, generally, more concerned with awareness than the other novels are. Despite the wide expanse of the setting and the great amount of extraneous material, the characters are far more conscious of themselves, and of others, than Hawthorne's characters have been previously. Their problems are personal, and though they are Hawthorne's old types and are not outstanding individualists, they are much more lively than the others. They do not merely exhibit the flow of passions and the urgency of forces greater than they.

Their awareness of one another in the *Marble Faun* is destructive. Individuality and mutual awareness, themes that result from Hawthorne's old concern with metaphysical forces and the new interest in human relations, the interest that leads to his use of characters who are out of control, combine to destroy happiness or contentment. High passion led to ruin in the *Scarlet Letter*. Individuality, that is. Here, though there is no inner monologue, the operation of one character on another is evident. Miriam's awareness of Hilda and Hilda's code of ethics influences her, little as she may approve of either. It is the extreme of awareness between Miriam and Kenyon that prevents him from hearing her confession and her from telling him her troubles. They fear each other's secrets and their beings. And all Donatello's story is one of gradual realization, from his perception of Miriam to his social awareness of guilt and crime. This change shows at once in the dialogue, from the first speeches after the murder to another change when Kenyon visits him, to another still in his resumption of a feigned innocence.

The awareness in general is emphasized by the numerous changes in character throughout the book, primarily in Donatello of course. But the problem for all of them, even Kenyon, is identity and place. The lack of it in general is emphasized both by the changes of dress and disguise and by the gradual creation of the work of art, which develops in its threefold stage and in its threefold materials and which is veiled or turned to the wall until revealed in the finished state of its being.

The theme of identity is associated, too, with both Hilda and Kenyon. These characters are all orphans; all, except Miriam, the most mysterious, are without family ties. Hilda, who seems so positively herself, has her own identity crisis. She is invited home by the Roman father, and there is something more than mere confusion in her claim, " 'I am a new creature . . .' " (vi, 415). Though Hilda is the least interesting and the most lifeless, it is precisely with her that Hawthorne's keenest awareness is displayed. In the episode of her confession, Hawthorne at one point, after gradual description of her actions and psychic state, actually comes just short of inner monologue (vi, 407), as was indicated in chapter 5.

In Donatello, Hawthorne again uses allegory, creating a situation and a representative man comparable to Goodman Brown. The quest for identity is forced upon Donatello from without, as with Adam in Eden. The quest theme appears in its basic form as Donatello becomes experienced, returns to his origins and takes his place, only to find that it is not his place, whereupon he gives up his identity by vanishing into a cell.

It can be no coincidence that, "It was difficult to make out the character of this young man" (vi, 28), not only in the comparison to the statue but in the attempt to mold a bust of him. The natural question is eventually asked by Miriam, " 'What are you, my friend?' " (vi, 98). Donatello replies soon afterwards, like Giovanni, by naming his name, " 'You are yourself, and I am Donatello . . .' " (vi, 99).

The ambiguities are symbols of Donatello's changing and developing identity. He is man, Adam out of the garden, Goodman Brown. For though he comes well-located in the past, he dwells in a mythical time just as he spent a past involved in myth. His moods, his character, may flash upon his face (VI, 33), but they are too mercurial to be caught until by chance Kenyon models the soul as the artist of "The Prophetic Pictures" does, by somehow seeing the character. Yet, the bust only abstracts, for Donatello continues to change, and no bust will reveal his character. And Hawthorne is describing a process, not characterizing a specific man. The point, if anything, is to show that character changes, that it cannot be defined, not to show what actually happens to a person called Donatello.

Compared with attempts to divine the character of Donatello, whose secrets would tell about man, the concern with Miriam's identity is more superficial. The mystery is outside her, as in Zenobia's case. Hawthorne's outstanding female characters are simply insoluble enigmas for both Hawthorne and his male characters. It may be expected, with all the rumors and with her mystery at the center of the action, that "nobody knew anything about Miriam" (VI, 35). The inevitable question eventually comes from her closest associates. Kenyon says, " 'Hilda, . . . who and what is Miriam?' " (VI, 132). The question here is about the eternal feminine, but it is not a question of consciousness or of character or of change, as with Donatello. The concern is more with the enigma of being than with identity. And the natural conclusion is the one Hilda states, " 'But she is such a mystery!' " (VI, 133). For the rest, Hawthorne continues with Miriam the study of motives that he began in creating Beatrice and repeated in the treatment of Zenobia. In a sense, he asks, in the long works, "What is Man?" and "What is Woman?" to conclude very little about either, except that it is all very strange.

Kenyon's failure to respond to Miriam's desire to confess is oversensitively Jamesian, in consonance with Hawthorne's theory of nonviolation. Too, however, his action suggests the refusal to involve himself with others, in part because of a fear of intimacy. The doctrine of nonviolation has become, in operation, a means not of preventing control alone but of preventing a person from giving the sympathy that another needs. One being is simply afraid of another when he has to come directly to face the mystery of being itself. More clearly in the *Marble Faun* than anywhere else in his work, Hawthorne animates shades. These persons are like Hester and Dimmesdale in being "awe-stricken" by their awareness of one another. Hawthorne anticipates the current dilemma in suggesting that the only thing they can offer one another—understanding—is not by any means enough.

The *Marble Faun* is a pessimistic book, in spite of its framework of orthodoxy. It criticizes all that it discusses: art, the past, the church, civilization. If Hawthorne intended the novel to be a philosophical book that deals with what is symbolized by the seven-branched candlestick of the Jews, it is Dionysiac and Nietzschean. Its constructiveness is by way of the negative. Hilda the Pure is the agent of as much trouble as that caused by the shadow and the past. She rejects Miriam, and Hawthorne makes it plain by repetition that Miriam's final loss of feminine restraint derives from the rejection, the scarlet woman driven away by the pious sister. Hilda causes the traduction of her code, and surely Hawthorne's condemnation of her is as strong as whatever sympathy he may have for her. Kenyon's reserve leaves Miriam bound and leads to her complicity in the act that Donatello performs.

There is no clear indication that the suffering is to accomplish anything. One may suggest that a doctrine of *felix culpa* is a despairing condemnation of all that one does not understand. Why the suffering? Why not innocence? The contrast between the innocence of Hilda and that of Donatello leaves us sympathizing with Donatello. He acts. Hilda only prays, egotistically, for cleansing. The world might have left the innocent alone. Instead, destruction of sin and crime is actually punished by the church as well as the state. Hypocrisy and disguise conceal the truth.

Life is destruction. Individuality is a challenge to fate; consciousness of the self is troublesome. Donatello becomes aware only to be destroyed. His individuality will be hidden in a monk's cowl, only replacing that of the shadow he threw from the precipice. The cowl is a disguise that covers all human frailties. The pilgrim goes in disguise not only because of his ego but also because he is nothing but his penances. He is always a sinner and may always be a criminal.

The vision of the *Marble Faun* is, after all, however, ironically affirmative, as Albert Camus' *The Plague* is affirmative when compared with his *The Stranger* or with John-Paul Sartre's *No Exit*. There is no Christian reaffirmation, nor any particular expression of faith in humanity. The affirmation is instead peaceful resolution, temporary cessation of tragedy. There is no hope, but there is human courage in the face of hopelessness. There are Hawthorne's old types. Kenyon assumes the anonymity of Walcott. Donatello and Miriam face the darkness, as Hester does. There is no hope, but there is relief in the conviction that artificial doctrines about sin and crime are not meaningful either. Donatello and Miriam have nothing to look forward to, but they are innocent of guilt.

Despite its fragmentary nature, *Doctor Grimshawe's Secret* includes Hawthorne's major themes, intensifies some of them, and to some extent suggests where Hawthorne would have gone in later development. With its many variations on themes of past and present, and old and new, this last novel presents a title character whose identity is not clear even to Hawthorne. And the implication is that both Grimshawe and Redclyffe resemble Fanshawe, of the earliest work, in that they are enigmas both to the reader and to themselves. More specifically, for Redclyffe, the problem is one of learning his origins. Thus, at the end of his career, in what is potentially his greatest work, Hawthorne is most explicit in dealing with a question that concerned him in his youth. In the last romances the question in all respects is a matter of identity and place. In what Edward Hutchins Davidson has published as the second draft, Ned puts to the doctor a version of the query that is at some time generated by the action with regard to most of Hawthorne's characters, " 'Then,

Dr. Grim,' said little Ned, 'tell me, in the first place, where I came from, and how you came to have me.' " [1] When the visiting representative of the English family sees the picture of a young man that Grimshawe has, he says, " 'Who was this man?' " (41) And Hawthorne uses his old theme of facial revelations in suggesting that the refined features reveal a man of high station. It is in part this method, used also in regard to his beauty, that suggests Ned's high origins. As in the *House of the Seven Gables*, there is much discussion of station and position, which have the capacity both to conceal and to reveal identity. But everyone has only vague origins in *Doctor Grimshawe's Secret*: Elsie, the doctor, Colgrave, even the Italian heir, who remarks to Redclyffe, " 'Like yourself, I am a hybrid . . .' " (136). Each, on the other hand, is related somehow to the long hereditary chain. Call it humanity in the abstract—where a spot is vacant. Hawthorne symbolizes it by the use of the vacant room and the vacant seat at table, by the footstep and the ancestral chair, again recalling the *House of the Seven Gables*. Still, the problem is to fill all the vacancies properly.

The potential greatness of *Doctor Grimshawe's Secret* is enhanced by Hawthorne's close intimacy with Redclyffe's very sensitive awareness. Hawthorne says at one point that the narrative will follow Redclyffe's consciousness. And though Hawthorne does not particularly do so where he proposes it, the point of view is limited to Redclyffe's consciousness. In sparing, but effective, use of inner monologue, Hawthorne now arrives at an intimacy that adds depth to the character he creates (59, 64).

A new dimension is added to *Doctor Grimshawe's Secret* in the use of memory, particularly associated with the Doppelgänger theme and the feeling of another self to be discovered. Memory also adds a new difficulty. Hawthorne makes it the technical source of his usual ambiguity and uses it to confuse the hero and complicate the search for identity that memory, in part, urges made. The use of memory adds a touch of the archetypal mythic element, one that Hawthorne obviously meant to emphasize. The unconscious Doppelgänger self, or the father image in the son, lies behind and beneath Redclyffe's quest, both complicating it and urging him to make it. Thus, Hawthorne demonstrates an awareness of much of what is often attributed to him as being used unconsciously. He knows that the problem is identity, that the search for origins is search for place, and that thorough identity is thorough nonentity. A parallel lies in the story of the twelve almoners, disciples, who have found nonentity in proving identity with the main line of the family.

And in *Doctor Grimshawe's Secret*, the theme of the search for the father recurs. Hawthorne had introduced the father-son theme in "Alice Doane's Appeal." The early picaresques emphasize the wanderer's lack of connections; he has only a guardian. "The Gentle Boy," if it can be typical, deals with a lone child. Robin seeks an uncle. In "Young Goodman Brown," ironically, the father symbol is at first the grandfather then the father, both of them the devil in disguise. Various aspects of the Doppelgänger theme suggest a father-son relationship. But after "Young Goodman Brown," the father-son theme is for the most part dropped, depending on whether *Septimius Felton* is considered an early or late work in conception. When Hawthorne returns to the theme in *Doctor Grimshawe's Secret*, he has the *Odyssey* as guide. The search is being made by both sides, by the son and by a representative of the family, though it may be significant that the father himself is dead.

But whatever his connections with the family, the vagaries of his recollections, discounting the possibility that he is completely wrong, cause Redclyffe to make the extensive search. The need to belong is great, and the place is vacant. But though the family have sought an heir they also have installed one, a usurper in a sense; perhaps they have provided a hostile father substitute, as in "Alice Doane's Appeal," or only a Judge Pyncheon to usurp Clifford's heritage. The true heir, even if Redclyffe was to be next in line, was apparently to be a gentle unknown old man, in a reversal of the technique used in "Young Good-man Brown," in which the helpful father was really the devil. Or perhaps both father and son are rejected, and their wish for unity maintains itself despite the family.

In *Doctor Grimshawe's Secret*, which might have been the most realistic of his novels, Hawthorne has used a good deal of allegory and myth. In a story where father and son are not individualized, Hawthorne operates with a version of the Christian myth of deity, in which father and son are one, or at least are urging toward each other in an aura combined of memory and the unconscious that emanates from the strivings of both together to be to-gether and be one. To the general search for home and place now is added search for ultimate origins—a heavenly place, it may be, ultimate home, utter form of home and utter being, paralleled on a lower plane by the relationship between England and America. There is a place for the heir on the right hand of the throne if he can manage to return to it. Indeed, the vacancy indicates full awareness of a break in the line. On simply a human level, it is very important to find an heir.

As the title indicates, *Doctor Grimshawe's Secret* too is a mystery tale, and one does not easily tell from the fragments whether Grimshawe's secret refers to the doctor himself primarily or to Redclyffe. The plans Hawthorne labors over suggest that it is Grimshawe's own secret, a theme that would have appealed to Hawthorne because it allowed him to show the extensive influence of one indi-vidual on the lives of others, perhaps violating their identi-ties, as Ethan Brand presumably does. But most of what is written, including the fragments published as the *Ances-tral Footstep*, suggests that Redclyffe's secret was the most important to Hawthorne and that Dr. Grimshawe's secret was what Redclyffe must find out in order to find out his own identity. The problem is getting the wise man's help, getting the prophecy from Tiresias. And the myth is repre-sented by the relationship between Redclyffe and Grim-shawe.

Grimshawe makes a jovial reply to Ned's question about

his identity. But Hawthorne appears to be serious, " 'Whence did you come? Whence did any of us come? Out of the darkness and mystery, out of nothingness, out of a kingdom of shadows; out of dust, clay, impure mud, I think, and to return to it again. Out of a former state of being, whence we have brought a good many shadowy recollections purporting that it was no very pleasant one. Out of a former life, of which this present one is the hell! And why are you come? Faith, Ned, he must be a wiser man than Doctor Grim who can tell why you, or any other mortal came hither; only one thing I [am] well aware of, it was not to be happy. To toil, and moil, and hope, and fear, and to love in a shadowy, doubtful sort of way, and to hate in bitter earnest—that is what you came for!' " (213). These sentiments also describe the metaphysics of Septimius, and both sentiments are surely autobiographical. The tone is that of mythic abstraction that Hawthorne sets for these fragments in his notes and in his handling of the various scenes in which Redclyffe is semiconscious. Redclyffe's semiconsciousness approximates what is now called the unconscious, as numerous passages reveal, particularly those that deal with Redclyffe's yearning to know where his origins are (145).

More than in earlier works, nevertheless reflecting the concern of the *House of the Seven Gables*, Hawthorne is concerned in these fragments with documents and hereditary books, written proof, positive knowledge, a scripture that establishes truth and distinguishes it from all the rumors and legends, and all the myths which surround Redclyffe's origins and his quest. The picture of the young man, another symbol of both identity and the unconscious, with its dubious capacity for revealing, as in Melville's *Pierre*, and variously elsewhere in Hawthorne, is one of the means by which Ned comes to dwell on thoughts of his origins. But the proofs are apparently no more valid than the rumors. Knowledge is impossible for all but the kind old man who, ironically, has known all along.

But Hawthorne apparently never intended Redclyffe to become the heir. He would leave England and his quest without knowing his origins. He would presumably have gone back to America with Elsie, as the new Adam, back to Paradise and nonentity, as was the case with Hawthorne's other reasonable young men. Perhaps. But if he had only remained ignorant of his origins, regardless of his future, he would represent the content of Grimshawe's remarks to Ned about the extent of man's knowledge of himself. The beginning and the end are hidden in mystery.

AT THE END of "Home Return," Oberon is quoted as
having written, "Soon to be all spirit, I have already a
spiritual sense of human nature, and see deeply into the
hearts of mankind, discovering what is hidden from the
wisest. . . . My glance comprehends the crowd, and
penetrates the breast of the solitary man" (XII, 41). The
passage not only reflects the concern with death that
appears earlier in *Fanshawe*; it also suggests that
Hawthorne was aware of an intuitive understanding of
human nature, the subject that he was to study in some
depth. The insight recorded in "The Birthmark" in the
commentary about Aylmer's dream, is an example, "Truth
often finds its way to the mind close muffled in robes of
sleep, and then speaks with uncompromising directness of
matters in regard to which we practise an unconscious
self-deception during our waking moments" (II, 52). This
shows the tyrannizing influence acquired by an idea, to
use Hawthorne's phraseology. Hawthorne's perceptions
are usually about human nature in general, not about
individual psychology, not about the subtleties of the
individual mind that make the character appear an individual. The individual, when he could not easily be categorized as a type, was and remained mysterious to
Hawthorne.

Hawthorne moves gradually toward the study of the
individual, at least toward a somewhat detached study of
himself, in the *Ancestral Footstep*. Yet, perhaps all his

work records the study of himself. A figure like Goodman Brown or Gervayse Hastings is both autobiographical and representative, a recognition that the deep personal experience may be so basically human as to be phylogenic. The greatness of these early stories derives from their having not allegorical but archetypal significance. If there was influence on these works, it probably was that of Greek tragedy, which used representative, masked, relatively uncharacterized figures motivated by forces that were mysterious. If this influence does not exist, Hawthorne's ability is the more remarkable.

Chronologically, on either side of the figure of Goodman Brown appear figures less impressive. Hawthorne but gradually acquired the combination of detachment and intimacy that resulted in "Young Goodman Brown." The allegorical figures and the types that follow Goodman Brown, influenced more perhaps by Molière than by Jonson, are in the old "humour" tradition. These figures are tyrannized by ideas that distort their actions and make them difficult to know as individuals.

Despite what Hawthorne may have achieved by the studies he made of indifference and distortion, he apparently decided to shift back to somewhat individualized figures and study them in action. He may have considered them as examples, instead of mere types, of human beings. His awareness of individuality as well as mystery is indicated by an observation that Holgrave makes to Phoebe about the inhabitants of an "odd and incomprehensible world." He says that "Men and women, and children, too, are such strange creatures, that one never can be certain that he really knows them; nor ever guess what they have been, from what he sees them to be now" (III, 214). In the apology that Coverdale makes for his analysis of Hollingsworth, the point is somewhat elaborated. Coverdale says that one should limit his study of individuals. If one studies himself too much the result is "diseased action of the heart." By the study of a character, we "insulate him from many of his true relations, magnify his peculiarities, inevitably tear him into parts, and, of course, patch him very clumsily together again," creating a monster. (III, 69).

Neither observation fully accounts for Hawthorne's methods of characterization. Coverdale is superficial, and he does not apologize for the intimate speculation about Zenobia. But "The Minister's Black Veil" indicates that Hawthorne had concluded that persons could not be known, because of their own veils and because of the limited perceptive ability of any observer. In addition, the pervasive influence of the irrational, as Hawthorne must have known, made any action seem more ambiguous than characteristic.

Coverdale's observation vaguely implies the concept of violation that attracted Hawthorne for a time in the middle of his career. The idea may be implied as early as the date of "Sylph Etherege" and "The Birthmark," before the notation in the notebooks in 1844 and the elaboration in "Ethan Brand." There is some question, however, as to how seriously Hawthorne propounded such a doctrine. He often enough shows violation, but he does not really have much to say about intellectual studies of the heart, not enough for criticism to have developed a head-heart psychology for him. Chillingworth's study, which is the most intense, is not indifferent. He violates and "sins" but Dimmesdale says that he and Hester have violated each other too. All the violation occurs within the artificial framework of social rules of behavior.

In "Rappaccini's Daughter," where violation occurs if anywhere, Hawthorne talks instead, superficially, about isolation. And Rappaccini's study is in any case not the important aspect of the story. If Rappaccini is important at all, it is as agent only, as old Moodie is in the *Blithedale Romance*. Violation in Hawthorne's work is the violation imposed by life and by interrelationships, as with Goodman Brown and Zenobia. Certainly figures are manipulated, and studied, but that is what Hawthorne does, not merely what his characters do. Real violation is done to Hester, Zenobia, and Miriam, to Robin and Goodman Brown, none of whom is made the object of an intellectual study of the heart. The theory, despite Coverdale's observation, probably had little influence on Hawthorne's characterization. Yet, of course the observations of both Coverdale and Holgrave are generally true, and they perhaps explain most of Hawthorne's difficulty.

Hawthorne, nevertheless, both studies and patches together, beginning at least as early as the date of "Rappaccini's Daughter." In the novels, he is concerned with interrelationships, adumbrated in "Sylph Etherege," one of the first of his works in which characters are not single-minded and masked. And in the novels he abundantly displays man's inhumanity to man. Here are violation, crime, isolation, depravity, indifference, unhappiness—and death. They are displayed, not self consciously moralized upon. With rare exceptions, the figures in the novels are communicative and sympathetic only in sin and crime, words, however, that ought not to be taken in a theological sense. For Hawthorne rarely condemns the actions of his characters. He does not even impute great crimes to Judge Pyncheon, and he does not make him pay. Society makes Hester and Donatello regret instinctive, natural, and innocent acts.

The novels study figures who interact with some degree of awareness of one another. But the study is still of human nature. Characters like Hester and Dimmesdale are motivated and manipulated by forces they do not understand, and the action takes place in an "incomprehensible world." The characters are inactive except when under outside control, as if the idea that distorts were now changed for a force that destroys. Figures like Zenobia and Hollingsworth, who may attempt to initiate action, are inevitably ruined. At first it may seem that Hawthorne suggests that individuality leads to destruction, but he appears instead to make the broader generalization that life leads to destruction.

The apparent conclusions are reached in the study of Miriam and Donatello. The question is, What is a person? On the morning after the murder, Miriam asks, " 'Am I not the same as yesterday?' " (vi, 242). She must be intensely aware of being the same, not because of an aberration that has allowed complicity, but because she is simply what she always was. She is at least used to herself. Miriam realizes that she has condoned the act and to that extent abetted, though perhaps what she feels is not a share in Donatello's guilt but only a share in his unhappiness. No legal cognizance is taken of her complicity.

Hilda, of course, from her immaculate position, will take cognizance of it. Insofar as Hawthorne can really sympathize with Hilda, he must condemn Miriam, though both Kenyon and Miriam remind Hilda that she is too pure, like the Archangel, for a practical ethic. But Miriam's question remains. How is she different from what she was on the day before the crime when Hilda loved her? How, for that matter, is Donatello different in character, basically? His remorse in fact suggests that he is as innocent as before but that he is now aware of crime, a blotch on his pride in his innocence. Awareness and pride are born together, as they were in Paradise. Both Miriam and Donatello continue to be sympathetically portrayed, and only Hilda and the state, the latter influenced by the special interest of the church, consider them guilty of anything more than a technical crime of passion. On both counts, technicality and passion, the crime can be excused. The act of murder was simple instinctive rejection of evil by people fundamentally good.

How much distance is there, then, between a person and the act he commits? To what extent is a person his acts? How much is a person what he seems? Who judges? To what extent can character be determined from acts, whether premeditated or impassioned? And if a person is not entirely his acts, is he responsible for either hypocrisy or crime? When these questions, and others that may occur, are put, how can one feel that he has any knowledge of what a person is? Does Hawthorne mean to suggest that Hilda is right and that Miriam is in fact as guilty as Donatello? Or is Donatello, or Hester, guilty of crime except by legal definition, which may be wrong? Can an act reveal anything, or is it not literally true that human action is meaningless? Miriam's consent, not an act perhaps but a failure to act, reveals nothing about her. Yet, she later feels her consent to have involved her—in what? If she feels involved in crime, it is because of her social and moral conditioning. At this point, we are involved, as Hawthorne was, in the confusion between language and action. Since presumably the concern is not with Miriam's remorse but with her instinctive consent, no connection between them is possible, and thus nothing is to be decided. Surely, it is at this conclusion, or one similar to it, that Hawthorne arrived when he thought about human nature. Such reflection easily led him to conclude that action was meaningless and that reform was useless since it could but impose artificial meaning, removing freedom. He does not propose a middle course; he proposes inaction in the face of utter bewilderment. There is nothing he knows to do. He is therefore completely agnostic, except in disapproving of action.

What is to conclude except what the Greeks concluded?—that when something occurred beyond the mean, an inexplicable and supernatural power was at work. If so, any individual is a combination that includes a patent unknown. He is never himself. He can never know himself. He is never the same. You never finish either characterizing him or talking about it. Definition is constantly beyond the resources of language, because it can never include the element of man's becoming.

Kenyon's attempt to model the bust of Donatello symbolizes the conclusion. A great change has occurred in Donatello, it seems. This much, as with Goodman Brown, is evident. Yet, the change is gradually less evident as the effect lessens. Donatello, perhaps affected by the realization of his coming punishment, even regains a touch of his former happiness. But the significant observation is that he changes so continually that he does not appear any self for a period long enough for a cast to be molded. Donatello, and everyone else, is too mercurial to characterize.

James finally solved Hawthorne's technical problem, along the lines set up by Hawthorne himself in the *Ances-*

tral Footstep. The move was of course to the inner monologue that accompanied complete author awareness and
complete sympathy with a character, at the sacrifice only
of the omniscient narrator for the limited point of view,
which perhaps compensated for the loss of omniscience.
Of course, this meant that each character was only another facet of the author's mind and of his imagination.
And with it went, when James achieved his greatest, the
concept and fact of the type character. Hawthorne accomplished something by his presentation of action—as in a
play—whereas James would have gone infinitesimally into
the mind. The Jamesian method would have limited
Hawthorne.

When one considers Hawthorne's view of human nature and human action, it seems inevitable that he should
urge an "age-long nap." His preoccupation with death,
which appears so often, both in his comments and in the
resolutions of his situations, is symbolized in the search for
home. Intermediate symbols recur in the themes of
houses, England, immortality, marriage, and identity. In
Our Old Home, at the end of the first sketch, Hawthorne
says, "I hope I do not compromise my American patriot-
ism by acknowledging that I was often conscious of a
fervent hereditary attachment to the native soil of our
forefathers, and felt it to be our own Old Home" (vii,
57). The statement is nearly impersonal in its truth. And
the truth seems to have been one of Hawthorne's earliest
feelings, as well as one of his latest. It pervades the *English Notebooks*. Experience of the desire to visit England
occurs as early as the conception of "Home Return,"
where he talks of a "homesickness for the
fatherland . . . which I yet believe that my peculiar in-
stinct impelled me to form, and upbraided me for not
accomplishing . . ." (xii, 26–27). Pearl's marriage to a
baronet was a projection of the "filial duty" mentioned
above.

Much of Hawthorne's interest may have derived from
the desire of the heir of a decayed family to visit the scene
of his origins in order to gain a measure of security. It was

also the act of an innocent and lonely youth, who had no father, to envelop himself in fantasies of a lost heritage; which also may have involved a desire for security. Certainly, the early sketches are more than autobiography. Like *Fanshawe*, which contains the earliest quest theme, they are dream projections that create an ideal. And the picaresque theme is enhanced by the overtone of myth that suggests that the early sketches expressed the unconscious if also the conscious.

Odyssey, place, identity, and home have occupied Hawthorne from the beginning. But the concept of home is fraught with meaning that lies deep. The picaresque and orphan themes of the early sketches culminate in the theme of a sketch appropriately called "Home Return." *Mosses From an Old Manse* takes its title from the name of a house, and so does the long introductory sketch to the *Scarlet Letter*. Robin searches for a house. Hawthorne's third novel is the *House of the Seven Gables. Our Old Home* is the title of a book that grows out of the *English Notebooks*; and *The Marble Faun* is "the romance of Monte Beni," Donatello's birthplace.

After the early picaresques, themes of identity and location become more overtly serious. One line of development goes through the more frenzied questing characters, where a personal concern is abstracted to the mythic level, in Goodman Brown, Reuben Bourne, Robin, and their like. Another line goes through Kenyon and Holgrave. The one group is actively prone to death, the other to anonymity. Holgrave "succeeds" to the traditional Hawthorne property. And the reabsorption prefigured in Pearl's marriage is realized, though ambiguously, in Septimius' heirdom. The ambiguity thereof derives not this time from Hawthorne's interest in vague knowledge but from his unwillingness to make the point outright. Also, if one may judge from the ending of *Doctor Grimshawe's Secret*, Hawthorne still had not found place himself. But this ending only helps the claimant to ease out of a difficulty. He does not want his claim proved, even if he would reject it. One wants and does not want immortality, a theme that seems to have been among Hawthorne's rejected plans. This theme of a lost inheritance begins early in "Home Return," where the narrator says that he will advise another young man that he is American, who, presumably, does not dwell upon the past and the loss.

The frenzied characters provide the greater art, from "Alice Doane's Appeal" to the *Scarlet Letter*. The other group leads, however, to the last fragments, to Redclyffe where the realistic and the mythic were to be combined, it seems, in what would most likely have been Hawthorne's great work. There, apparently, he meant to analyze the problem of past and present, father and son, origin and place, self and other, on all levels. The resolution of those various questions probably would have been that identity could not be known and that place was nonexistence. The first is a logical result both of Hawthorne's own failure in the search and of his gradual realization that character was not to be portrayed without distortion. The other was his personal inclination in a universe that made human life seem grotesque and human action valueless. If he chose two lines, the reasonable and the frenzied, it was perhaps because he maintained his dichotomy, being Man Thinking, of the pragmatic and the transcendental, the novel and the romance, the real and the ideal; agnosticism, in short, which Hawthorne probably thought the only reasonable approach to metaphysics and, so far as possible, when one lives, also to life.

Two secondary themes had been in Hawthorne's mind for a long time before he wrote the fragments. One is that introduced in the *American Notebooks*, and used in "The Old Manse," of the house that has grown by accretion from one generation to another. He noted this also in the *English Notebooks* and in the fragments, and earlier in the *House of the Seven Gables*. The symbol is of the accretion of generations, heaping up the dead, putting them neatly and finally in place. The other theme is that of a footprint, and Hawthorne must have been elated at recalling, when in England, his notation in the American journals, "The print in blood of a naked foot to be traced through the street of a town" (IX, 395). Footsteps throughout Hawthorne's work are the indication of presence, and the suggestion is that the presence is more than it seems. To have ended with Septimius' walking and with Redclyffe's measuring his foot against that on the step of the porch seems aesthetically sufficient. Symbolically, the machinery is transcendent. And both themes lead to location.

Though these are minor themes, they indicate the unconscious and intuitive depth of Hawthorne's concern with home and with England as an intermediate symbol of home. After the novels, come the fragments with their varying treatments of the themes of England and America as well as themes of ancestry and home. In *Septimius Felton*, for example, where the theme of home develops within the setting of the Revolutionary War, the attraction to England is strong enough to draw Septimius there. The concerns of the early sketches have become obsessive, and it probably is not by chance that *Septimius Felton* is set at the time of the War, when the break with home was made.

Hawthorne's treatment of the question of immortality has at least two aspects. If, after having the matter argued at length in *Septimius Felton*, he intended what occurred to Septimius, his reasonable abandonment of the idea, then Hawthorne has again decided in favor of easeful death. Such immortality as may be is provided by the continuation of the lineage. It must be noted, however, that Hawthorne stopped short of this, for most of his characters do not have children. Except for such figures as Goodman Brown whose children are mentioned incidentally, only Pearl, among the important characters, becomes a parent. Pearl's parenthood may be disregarded, because she is a woman, because the ending is not logical, or, if nothing else, because Pearl has already lost her name in her baronetcy. What matters is that Fanshawe and Septimius have none. Reuben Bourne's only son dies by his father's hand. Ethan has none. Not even Holgrave, Kenyon or Walcott has children. Thus, location in the ancestral line is accession to death. And the ordinary characters in *Septimius Felton* argue in favor of death.

On the other hand, Hawthorne is occupied all his life with the theme of immortality. Perhaps he was quite serious about the argument that Septimius makes in favor of it. But, if so, the point is to live forever, not a theological point of Christian immortality, for example. And such arguments as Hawthorne presents through Septimius are, if more than noncommital, then anti-Christian and anti-Nature. The question is whether Hawthorne's wish for immortality affects the thesis that he wishes for death himself and urges it on his characters. The simplest and perhaps truest reply is to refuse to admit that the questions are related. For a desire for peace in death has not of necessity anything to do with the wish to live forever. The latter, ironically, seems to show in Hawthorne a strong tendency to reform, while it also suggests again the uselessness of human life. One may suggest that in Hawthorne's work the questions of immortality and the desire for death did, in fact, have nothing to do with each other. Immortality is a dream, death is a fact.

But the desire for immortality is, in any case, a desire for eternal consciousness of eternal place and eternity above the search for place, narcissistic and prideful desire for complete awareness. Thus, the novel fragments more explicitly state and more strongly imply what Hawthorne's doctrine of home means: the desire for peace in nonexistence. In Fanshawe's death, in the Oberon papers, in "Monsieur du Miroir," in "P's Correspondence" and in Zenobia's death scene, Hawthorne expresses the desire to die and be aware of it. It is the peace without the loss of consciousness, desire to taste of the tree in Eden, that is longed for.

A passage from the *American Notebooks*, used in the *Scarlet Letter* (1, 188), seems like a very personal statement, "In moods of heavy despondency, one feels as if it would be delightful to sink down in some quiet spot, and lie there forever, letting the soil gradually accumulate and form a little hillock over us, and the grass and perhaps flowers gather over it. At such times, death is too much of an event to be wished for;—we have not spirits to encounter it; but choose to pass out of existence in this sluggish way" (102).

Hawthorne says in the *American Notebooks* that "Every individual has a place to fill . . ." (ix, 32). That is, the fact that he exists means something. But there is very little suggestion in Hawthorne's work that finding place in society is to make a man whole. Instead, it will provide him with anonymity. He will escape the struggle and pain of life and find peace only in this kind of nonexistence—perhaps. A man's only other choice is death. Existence is a great pain, Hawthorne suggests, and life is distortion of chaos.

NOTES

MOST REFERENCES are in the text itself. References to the notebooks of Hawthorne are to the editions by Randall Stewart, which are identified, as are all the other items mentioned, in the bibliography. References are occasionally made to notebook passages found only in Volume IX of the Riverside Edition, since they were omitted from Stewart's edition of the *American Notebooks*. These, with the exception of pages 395–97 of Volume IX, are listed in Stewart's preface to the *American Notebooks*. References to Hawthorne's works are made to the first two volumes of the Centenary Edition published by the Ohio State University Press. These are Volume I, the *Scarlet Letter*, and Volume III, the *Blithedale Romance and Fanshawe*. Volume II, containing the *House of the Seven Gables*, was published too recently for references to be made to it. References to other works by Hawthorne are to the Riverside Edition, published by Houghton Mifflin. References to Edward Hutchins Davidson's edition of *Dr. Grimshawe's Secret* are identified where they first begin to appear in the text.

1 — The Context

1. M. L. Kesselring, *Hawthorne's Reading, 1828–1850* (New York City: The New York Public Library, 1949).

2. Régis Michaud, *The American Novel Today; A Social and Psychological Study* (Boston: Little, Brown, and Company, 1928), p. 38.

3. Vladimir Astrov, "Hawthorne and Dostoevski as Explorers of the Human Conscience," *New England Quarterly*, xv (1942), 296–319; C. A. Manning, "Hawthorne and Dostoyevsky," *Slavonic Review*, xiv (1936), 417–24.

4. Andrew Schiller, "The Moment and the Endless Voyage: A Study of Hawthorne's 'Wakefield,'" *Diameter*, 1 (1951), 7.

5. Homer, *The Odyssey*, trans. Robert Fitzgerald (New York: Doubleday and Company, Anchor Books, 1961), p. 118.

6. *Ibid.*, p. 356.

7. *Ibid.*, p. 357.

8. James K. Folsom, *Man's Accidents and God's Purposes; Multiplicity in Hawthorne's Fiction* (New Haven, College and University Press, 1963).

2—The Narrative Masks

1. Johann Wolfgang von Goethe, *Wilhelm Meister's Apprenticeship*, trans. Thomas Carlyle (New York: Collier Books, 1962), p. 114.

5—Search for Awareness

1. Johann Wolfgang von Goethe, *Wilhelm Meister's Apprenticeship*, trans. Thomas Carlyle (New York: Collier Books, 1962), p. 405.

2. *Ibid.*, p. 406.

3. *Hawthorne's Doctor Grimshawe's Secret*, ed. Edward Hutchins Davidson (Cambridge, Massachusetts: Harvard University Press, 1954), p. 163.

6—Representative and Allegorical Men

1. Edward Hutchins Davidson, *Hawthorne's Last Phase* (New Haven: Yale University Press, 1949), p. 84.

2. B. Bernard Cohen, "*Paradise Lost* and 'Young Goodman Brown,'" Essex Institute *Historical Collections*, XCIV (1958), 282–96; E. A. Robinson, "The Vision of Goodman Brown: A Source and Interpretation," *American Literature*, XXXV (1963), 218–25.

3. Davidson, p. 82.

7—Who is Beatrice?

1. Benjamin Rush, "Observations and Reasoning in Medicine," in Russell B. Nye and Norman S. Grabo, eds. *Ameri-*

can Thought and Writing, Vol. II (Boston: Houghton Mifflin Co., 1965), pp. 196–203.

10—Who are Zenobia and Miriam?

1. *Hawthorne's Doctor Grimshawe's Secret,* ed. Edward Hutchins Davidson (Cambridge, Massachusetts: Harvard University Press, 1954), p. 213.

A SELECTED BIBLIOGRAPHY

PROJECTS FOR Hawthorne bibliographies have unfortunately not materialized. Miss Beatrice Ricks of Central Missouri State College now has a comprehensive bibliography of secondary materials on Hawthorne, including even the nineteenth-century material. It deserves and needs to be published.

The following bibliography was prepared just before printing and thus includes recent items which, however, could not have been noted in the text. Though I also now have a nearly complete bibliography of the twentieth-century materials on Hawthorne and have seen most of the items, I have selected on the basis of availability. Fortunately, much of the best secondary material on Hawthorne has been published in the easily available major journals. Yet, important items are omitted from the list below because they appear in publications not now available for checking. In addition, nearly all source studies are omitted, though some are quite valuable. There is abundant room for a long monograph on Hawthorne's sources and on the related subject of parallels and relationships. Too, the many articles dealing with biography have been omitted from the following list, leaving for the most part, however, a good selection of articles and books that interpret Hawthorne's work.

Abel, Darrel. "Hawthorne's Dimmesdale: Fugitive from Wrath," *Nineteenth-Century Fiction*, XI (1956), 81–105.
———. "Hawthorne's Hester," *College English*, XIII (1952), 303–9.
———. "Hawthorne's House of Tradition," *South Atlantic Quarterly*, LII (1953), 561–78.

Abel, Darrel. "Hawthorne's Pearl: Symbol and Character," *English Literary History*, XVIII (1951), 50–66.

———. "Hawthorne's Skepticism about Social Reform: With Especial Reference to *The Blithedale Romance*," *University of Kansas City Review*, XIX (1953), 181–93.

———. "The Theme of Isolation in Hawthorne," *Personalist*, XXXII (1951), 42–49, 182–90.

Anderson, D. K. Jr. "Hawthorne's Crowds," *Nineteenth-Century Fiction*, VII (1952), 39–50.

Arden, Eugene. "Hawthorne's 'Case of Arthur D.,' " *American Imago*, XVIII (1961), 45–55.

Arvin, Newton. *Hawthorne*. Boston: Little, Brown and Company, 1929. Reprinted by Russell and Russell, New York, 1961.

Askew, Melvin W. "Hawthorne, the Fall, and the Psychology of Maturity," *American Literature*, XXXIV (1962), 335–43.

Astrov, Vladimir. "Hawthorne and Dostoevski as Explorers of the Human Conscience," *New England Quarterly*, XV (1942), 296–319.

Austin, Allen. "Distortion in 'The (Complete) *Scarlet Letter*,' " *College English*, XXIII (1961), 61–62.

———. "Hester Prynne's Plan of Escape: The Moral Problem," *University of Kansas City Review*, XXVIII (1962), 317–18.

———. "Satire and Theme in *The Scarlet Letter*," *Philological Quarterly*, XLI (1962), 508–11.

Baskett, Sam S. "*The* (Complete) *Scarlet Letter*," *College English*, XXII (1961), 321–28.

Beebe, Maurice. "The Fall of the House of Pyncheon," *Nineteenth-Century Fiction*, XI (1956), 1–17.

Bell, Millicent. *Hawthorne's View of the Artist*. New York: State University of New York, 1962.

Bewley, Marius. *The Complex Fate: Hawthorne, Henry James and Some Other American Writers*. London: Chatto and Windus, 1952.

Bicknell, John W. "*The Marble Faun* Reconsidered," *University of Kansas City Review*, XX (1954), 193–99.

Birdsall, Virginia Ogden. "Hawthorne's Fair-Haired Maidens: The Fading Light," *PMLA*, LXXV (1960), 250–56.

———. "Hawthorne's Oak Tree Image," *Nineteenth-Century Fiction*, XV (1960), 181–85.

Blair, Walter. "Color, Light and Shadow in Hawthorne's Fiction," *New England Quarterly*, XV (1942), 74–94.

⸺. "Hawthorne," in *Eight American Authors: A Review of Research and Criticism*. ed. Floyd Stovall. New York: The Modern Language Association of America, 1956.

Bode, Carl. "Hawthorne's *Fanshawe*: The Promising of Greatness," *New England Quarterly*, xxiii (1950), 235–42.

Boewe, Charles. "Rappaccini's Garden," *American Literature*, xxx (1958), 37–49.

Bonham, Sister M. Hilda. "Hawthorne's Symbols *Sotto Voce*," *College English*, xx (1959), 184–86.

Brennan, Joseph X. and Seymour L. Gross. "The Origin of Hawthorne's Unpardonable Sin," *Boston University Studies in English*, iii (1957), 123–29.

Brodtkorb, Paul Jr., "Art Allegory in *The Marble Faun*," *PMLA*, lxxvii (1962), 254–67.

Broes, Arthur T. "Journey into Moral Darkness: 'My Kinsman, Major Molineux' as Allegory," *Nineteenth-Century Fiction*, xix (1964), 171–84.

Brown, E. K. "Hawthorne, Melville and 'Ethan Brand,'" *American Literature*, iii (1931), 72–75.

Brown, Merle E. "The Structure of *The Marble Faun*," *American Literature*, xxviii (1956), 302–13.

Burhans, Clinton S. Jr. "Hawthorne's Mind and Art in 'The Hollow of the Three Hills,'" *Journal of English and Germanic Philology*, lx (1961), 286–95.

Cargill, Oscar. "Nemesis and Nathaniel Hawthorne," *PMLA*, lii (1937), 848–62.

Carpenter, Frederic I. "Puritans Preferred Blondes: The Heroines of Melville and Hawthorne," *New England Quarterly*, ix (1936), 253–72.

⸺. "Scarlet A Minus," *College English*, v (1944), 173–80.

Cecil, L. Moffitt. "Hawthorne's Optical Device," *American Quarterly*, xv (1963), 76–84.

Charney, Maurice. "Hawthorne and the Gothic Style," *New England Quarterly*, xxxiv (1961), 36–49.

Cochran, Robert W. "Hawthorne's Choice: The Veil or the Jaundiced Eye," *College English*, xxiii (1962), 342–46.

Cohen, B. Bernard. "*Paradise Lost* and 'Young Goodman Brown,'" *Essex Institute Historical Collections*, xciv (1958), 282–96.

Connolly, Thomas E. "Hawthorne's 'Young Goodman Brown': An Attack on Puritanic Calvinism," *American Literature*," xxviii (1956), 370–75.

Connolly, Thomas E. "How Young Goodman Brown Became Old Badman Brown," *College English,* XXIV (1962), 153.

Connors, Thomas E. " 'My Kinsman, Major Molineux': A Reading," *Modern Language Notes,* LXXIV (1959), 299–302.

Cowley, Malcolm. "Five Acts of *The Scarlet Letter*," *College English,* XIX (1957), 11–16.

———. "Hawthorne in the Looking-Glass," *Sewanee Review,* LVI (1948), 545–63.

Crews, Frederick C. *The Sins of the Fathers; Hawthorne's Psychological Themes.* New York: Oxford University Press, 1966.

Dauner, Louise. "The 'Case' of Tobias Pearson: Hawthorne and the Ambiguities," *American Literature,* XXI (1950), 464–72.

Davidson, Edward H. "Dimmesdale's Fall," *New England Quarterly,* XXXVI (1963), 358–70.

———. *Hawthorne's Last Phase.* New Haven, Conn.: Yale University Press, 1949.

Davidson, Frank. "Hawthorne's Hive of Honey," *Modern Language Notes,* LXI (1946), 14–21.

———. "Toward a Re-Evaluation of *The Blithedale Romance*," *New England Quarterly,* XXV (1952), 374–83.

———. " 'Young Goodman Brown'—Hawthorne's Intent," *Emerson Society Quarterly,* No. 31 (1963), pp. 68–71.

Dichmann, Mary E. "Hawthorne's 'Prophetic Pictures,' " *American Literature,* XXIII (1951), 188–202.

Dillingham, William B. "Structure and Theme in *The House of the Seven Gables*," *Nineteenth-Century Fiction,* XIV (1959), 59–70.

Donohue, Agnes McNeill. *A Casebook on the Hawthorne Question.* New York: Thomas Y. Crowell Company, 1963.

———. " 'From Whose Bourn No Traveller Returns': A Reading of 'Roger Malvin's Burial,' " *Nineteenth-Century Fiction,* XVIII (1963), 1–19.

Doubleday, Neal F. "Hawthorne and Literary Nationalism," *American Literature,* XII (1941), 447–53.

———. "Hawthorne's Use of Three Gothic Patterns," *College English,* VII (1946), 250–62.

———. "The Theme of Hawthorne's 'Fancy's Show Box,' " *American Literature,* X (1938), 341–43.

Durr, Robert A. *Hawthorne's Ironic Mode*," *New England Quarterly,* XXX (1957), 486–95.

Edgren, C. Hobart. "Hawthorne's 'The Ambitious Guest': An Interpretation," *Nineteenth-Century Fiction*, x (1955), 151–56.

Eisinger, Chester E. "Hawthorne as Champion of the Middle Way," *New England Quarterly*, xxvii (1954), 27–52.

Evans, Oliver. "Allegory and Incest in 'Rappaccini's Daughter,'" *Nineteenth-Century Fiction*, xix (1964), 185–95.

———. "The Cavern and the Fountain: Paradox and Double Paradox in 'Rappaccini's Daughter,'" *College English*, xxiv (1963), 461–63.

Fairbanks, Henry G. 'Hawthorne amid the Alien Corn," *College English*, xvii (1956), 263–68.

———. "Hawthorne and the Machine Age," *American Literature*, xxviii (1956), 155–63.

———. "Man's Separation from Nature: Hawthorne's Philosophy of Suffering and Death," *Christian Scholar*, xlii (1959), 51–63.

———. "Sin, Free Will, and 'Pessimism' in Hawthorne," *PMLA*, lxxi (1956), 975–89.

Fogle, Richard H. *Hawthorne's Fiction: The Light and the Dark*. Revised Edition. Norman, Oklahoma: The University of Oklahoma Press, 1964.

Folsom, James K. *Man's Accidents and God's Purposes: Multiplicity in Hawthorne's Fiction*. New Haven, Connecticut: College and University Press, 1963.

Foster, Charles H. "Hawthorne's Literary Theory," *PMLA*, lvii (1942), 241–54.

Gargano, J. W. "Hawthorne's 'The Artist of the Beautiful,'" *American Literature*, xxxv (1963), 225–30.

Garlitz, Barbara. "Pearl: 1850–1955," *PMLA*, lxxii (1957), 689–99.

Gerber, John C. "Form and Content in *The Scarlet Letter*," *New England Quarterly*, xvii (1944), 25–55.

Granger, Bruce I. "Arthur Dimmesdale as Tragic Hero," *Nineteenth-Century Fiction*, xix (1964), 197–203.

Griffith, Clark, "Substance and Shadow: Language and Meaning in *The House of the Seven Gables*," *Modern Philology*, li (1953), 187–95.

Gross, Robert. "Hawthorne's First Novel: The Future of a Style," *PMLA*, lxxviii (1963), 60–68.

Gross, Seymour L., ed. *A Scarlet Letter Handbook*. San Francisco: Wadsworth Publishing Company, 1960.

———. "Hawthorne's 'Alice Doane's Appeal,'" *Nineteenth-Century Fiction*, x (1955), 232–36.

Gross, Seymour L. "Hawthorne's Moral Realism," *Emerson Society Quarterly*, No. 25 (1961), 11–13.

——. "Hawthorne's 'My Kinsman, Major Molineux': History as Moral Adventure," *Nineteenth-Century Fiction*, XII (1957), 97–109.

Gwynn, Frederick L. "Hawthorne's 'Rappaccini's Daughter,' " *Nineteenth-Century Fiction*, VII (1952), 217–19.

Haugh, Robert F. "The Second Secret in *The Scarlet Letter*," *College English*, XVII (1956), 269–71.

Havens, Elmer A. "The 'Golden Branch' as Symbol in *The House of the Seven Gables*," *Modern Language Notes*, LXXIV (1959), 20–22.

Hawthorne, Nathaniel. *The American Notebooks by Nathaniel Hawthorne.* ed. Randall Stewart. New Haven: Yale University Press, 1932.

——. *The Centenary Edition of Hawthorne's Works.* Ed. William Charvat, *et al.* Columbus, Ohio: Ohio University Press, 1962——.

——. *The English Notebooks by Nathaniel Hawthorne.* Ed. Randall Stewart. New York: Modern Language Association of America, 1941.

——. *Hawthorne's Doctor Grimshawe's Secret.* Ed. Edward H. Davidson. Cambridge, Massachusetts: Harvard University Press, 1954.

——. *The Works of Nathaniel Hawthorne.* 15 vols. Boston and New York: Houghton, Mifflin and Company, Riverside Edition (variously listed dates).

Hedges, William L. "Hawthorne's *Blithedale*: The Function of the Narrator," *Nineteenth-Century Fiction*, XIV (1960), 303–16.

Heilman, R. B. "Hawthorne's 'The Birthmark': Science as Religion," *South Atlantic Quarterly*, XLVIII (1949), 575–83.

Hoeltje, Hubert H. *Inward Sky: The Mind and Art of Nathaniel Hawthorne.* Durham, North Carolina: Duke University Press, 1962.

Hoffman, Daniel G. "Yankee Bumpkin and Scapegoat King," *Sewanee Review*, LXIX (1961), 48–60.

Hovey, Richard B. "Love and Hate in 'Rappaccini's Daughter,' " *University of Kansas City Review*, XXIX (1962), 137–45.

Howard, Leon. "Hawthorne's Fiction," *Nineteenth-Century Fiction*, VII (1953), 237–50.

James, Henry. *Hawthorne*. London: Macmillan, 1879.

Jordan, Gretchen G. "Hawthorne's 'Bell': Historical Evolution through Symbol," *Nineteenth-Century Fiction*, XIX (1964), 123–39.

Joseph, Brother. "Art and Event in *Ethan Brand*," (sic) *Nineteenth-Century Fiction*, XV (1960), 249–57.

Kariel, Henry S. "Man Limited: Nathaniel Hawthorne's Classicism," *South Atlantic Quarterly*, LII (1953), 528–42.

Laser, Marvin. " 'Head,' 'Heart,' and 'Will' in Hawthorne's Psychology," *Nineteenth-Century Fiction*, X (1955), 130–40.

Leavis, Q. D. "Hawthorne As Poet," *Sewanee Review*, LIX Part I (Spring, 1951), pp. 179–205; Part II (Summer, 1951), pp. 426–58.

Lesser, Simon O. "The Image of the Father: A Reading of 'My Kinsman, Major Molineux' and 'I Want to Know Why,' " *Partisan Review*, XXII (1955), 372–90.

Levin, David. "Shadows of Doubt: Specter Evidence in Hawthorne's 'Young Goodman Brown,' " *American Literature*, XXXIV (1962), 344–52.

Levin, Harry. *The Power of Blackness: Hawthorne, Poe, Melville*. New York: Vintage Books, 1960.

Levy, Alfred J. *"The House of the Seven Gables:* The Religion of Love," *Nineteenth-Century Fiction*, XVI (1961), 189–203.

Levy, Leo B. "Hawthorne's 'Middle Ground,' " *Studies in Short Fiction*, II (1964), 56–60.

Luecke, Sister Jane Marie, O. S. B. "Villains and Non-Villains in Hawthorne's Fiction," *PMLA*, LXXVIII (1963), 551–58.

Lynch, James J. "Structure and Allegory in 'The Great Stone Face,' " *Nineteenth-Century Fiction*, XV (1960), 137–46.

McCabe, Bernard. "Narrative Technique in 'Rappaccini's Daughter,' " *Modern Language Notes*, LXXIV (1959), 213–17.

McCullen, Joseph T. and John C. Guilds. "The Unpardonable Sin in Hawthorne: A Re-Examination," *Nineteenth-Century Fiction*, XV (1960), 221–37.

McKeithan, D. M. "Hawthorne's 'Young Goodman Brown': An Interpretation," *Modern Language Notes*, LXVII (1952), 93–96.

MacLean, Hugh N. "Hawthorne's *Scarlet Letter:* 'The Dark Problem of This Life,' " *American Literature*, XXVII (1955), 12–24.

McNamara, Anne Marie. "The Character of Flame: The Function of Pearl in *The Scarlet Letter*," *American Literature*, XXVII (1956), 537–53.

Male, Roy R. "Hawthorne's Allegory of Guilt and Redemption," *Emerson Society Quarterly*, No. 25 (1961), 16–18.

Male, Roy R. Jr. *Hawthorne's Tragic Vision.* Austin: University of Texas Press, 1957.

Manning, C. A. "Hawthorne and Dostoyevsky," *Slavonic Review*, XIV (1936), 417–24.

Marcus, Fred H. "*The Scarlet Letter*: The Power of Ambiguity," *English Journal*, LI (1962), 449–58.

Marks, Alfred H. "Two Rodericks and Two Worms: 'Egotism; or, The Bosom Serpent' as Personal Satire," *PMLA*, LXXIV (1959), 607–12.

Marks, Alfred H. "Who Killed Judge Pyncheon? The Role of the Imagination in *The House of the Seven Gables*," *PMLA*, LXXI (1956), 355–69.

Marks, Barry A. "The Origin of Original Sin in Hawthorne's Fiction," *Nineteenth-Century Fiction*, XIV (1960), 359–62.

Mathews, James W. "Hawthorne and the Chain of Being," *Modern Language Quarterly*, XVIII (1957), 282–94.

Matthiessen, F. O. *American Renaissance; Art and Expression in the Age of Emerson and Whitman.* New York: Oxford University Press, 1941.

Michaud, Régis. *The American Novel Today; A Social and Psychological Study.* Boston: Little, Brown, and Company, 1928.

Miller, James E. Jr. "Hawthorne and Melville: The Unpardonable Sin," *PMLA*, LXX (1955), 91–114.

Miller, Paul W. "Hawthorne's 'Young Goodman Brown': Cynicism or Meliorism?" *Nineteenth-Century Fiction*, XIV (1959), 255–64.

Moss, Sidney P. "The Problem of Theme in *The Marble Faun*," *Nineteenth-Century Fiction*, XVIII (1964), 393–99.

Newman, Franklin B. " 'My Kinsman, Major Molineaux': (sic) An Interpretation," *University of Kansas City Review*, XXI (1955), 203–12.

Nolte, W. H. "Hawthorne's Dimmesdale: A Small Man Gone Wrong," *New England Quarterly*, XXXVIII (1965), 168–86.

Normand, Jean. *Nathaniel Hawthorne: Esquisse d'une analyse de la création artistique.* Paris: Presses Univers. de France, 1964.

O'Donnell, Charles R. "Hawthorne and Dimmesdale: The Search for the Realm of Quiet," *Nineteenth-Century Fiction,* xiv (1960), 317–32.

Orel, Harold. "The Double Symbol," *American Literature,* xxiii (1951), 1–6.

Orians, Harrison G. "Hawthorne and 'The Maypole of Merry Mount,'" *Modern Language Notes,* liii (1938), 159–67.

Paul, Louis. "A Psychoanalytic Reading of Hawthorne's 'Major Molineux': The Father Manqué and the Protégé Manqué," *American Imago,* xviii (1961), 279–88.

Pearce, Roy Harvey. "Hawthorne and the Sense of the Past, or, The Immortality of Major Molineux," *Journal of English Literary History,* xxi (1954), 327–49.

————, ed. *Hawthorne Centenary Essays.* Columbus, Ohio: Ohio University Press, 1964.

————. "Robin Molineux on the Analyst's Couch: A Note on the Limits of Psychoanalytic Criticism," *Criticism,* i (1959), 83–90.

√Price, S. R. "The Heart, the Head and 'Rappaccini's Daughter,'" *New England Quarterly,* xxvii (1954), 399–403.

Ragan, James F. "The Irony in Hawthorne's Blithedale," *New England Quarterly,* xxxv (1962), 239–46.

Ringe, Donald A. "Hawthorne's Psychology of the Head and Heart," *PMLA,* lxv (1950), 120–32.

Robinson, E. A. "The Vision of Goodman Brown: A Source and Interpretation," *American Literature,* xxxv (1963), 218–25.

Rosenberry, Edward H. "Hawthorne's Allegory of Science: 'Rappaccini's Daughter,'" *American Literature,* xxxii (1960), 39–46.

Sampson, Edward C. "Motivation in *The Scarlet Letter,*" *American Literature,* xxviii (1957), 511–13.

Sandeen, Ernest. "*The Scarlet Letter* as a Love Story," *PMLA,* lxxvii (1962), 425–35.

Schiller, Andrew. "The Moment and the Endless Voyage: A Study of Hawthorne's 'Wakefield,'" *Diameter,* i (1951), 7–12.

Schwartz, Joseph. "A Note on Hawthorne's Fatalism" *Modern Language Notes,* lxx (1955), 33–36.

————. "'Ethan Brand' and the Natural Goodness of Man: A Phenomenological Inquiry," *Emerson Society Quarterly,* No. 39 (1965), pp. 78–81.

————. "Myth and Ritual in *The Marble Faun,*" *Emerson Society Quarterly,* No. 25 (1961), 26–29.

Schwartz, Joseph. "Three Aspects of Hawthorne's Puritanism," *New England Quarterly*, XXXVI (1963), 192–208.

Scott, Arthur L. "The Case of the Fatal Antidote," *Arizona Quarterly*, XI (1955), 38–43.

Scrimgeour, Gary J. "*The Marble Faun*: Hawthorne's Faery Land," *American Literature*, XXXVI (1964), 271–87.

Shroeder, John W. "Hawthorne's 'Egotism; or, The Bosom Serpent' and Its Source," *American Literature*, XXXI (1959), 150–62.

———. " 'That Inward Sphere': Notes on Hawthorne's Heart Imagery and Symbolism," *PMLA*, LXV (1950), 106–19.

Stanton, Robert. "Dramatic Irony in Hawthorne's Romances," *Modern Language Notes*, LXXI (1956), 420–26.

———. "The Trial of Nature: An Analysis of *The Blithedale Romance*," *PMLA*, LXXVI (1961), 528–38.

Stein, William Bysshe. " 'The Artist of the Beautiful': Narcissus and the Thimble," *American Imago*, XVIII (1961), 35–44.

———. *Hawthorne's Faust: A Study of the Devil Archetype*. Gainesville, Florida: University of Florida Press, 1953.

———. "The Parable of the Antichrist in 'The Minister's Black Veil,' " *American Literature*, XXVII (1955), 386–92.

Stewart, Randall. *Nathaniel Hawthorne, A Biography*. New Haven, Connecticut: Yale University Press, 1948.

Stibitz, E. Earle. "Ironic Unity in Hawthorne's 'The Minister's Black Veil,' " *American Literature*, XXXIV (1962), 182–90.

Stone, Edward. "The Antique Gentility of Hester Prynne," *Philological Quarterly*, XXXVI (1957), 90–96.

Strauch, Carl F. "The Problem of Time and the Romantic Mode in Hawthorne, Melville, and Emerson," *Emerson Society Quarterly*, No. 35 (1964), pp. 50–60.

Tanselle, G. Thomas. "A Note on the Structure of *The Scarlet Letter*," *Nineteenth-Century Fiction*, XVII (1962), 283–85.

Thompson, W. R. "Theme and Method in Hawthorne's 'The Great Carbuncle,' " *South-Central Bulletin*, XXI, iv (1961), 3–10.

Thorslev, Peter L. Jr. "Hawthorne's Determinism: An Analysis," *Nineteenth-Century Fiction*, XIX (1964) 141–57.

Turner, Arlin. "Hawthorne and Reform," *New England Quarterly*, xv (1942), 700–714.

———. "Hawthorne's Literary Borrowings," *PMLA*, LI (1936), 543–62.

———. *Nathaniel Hawthorne; An Introduction and Interpretation*. New York: Barnes and Nobel, 1961.

———. "Nathaniel Hawthorne in American Studies," *College English*, XXVI (1964), 133–39.

Vanderbilt, Kermit. "The Unity of Hawthorne's 'Ethan Brand,' " *College English*, XXIV (1963), 453–56.

Van Doren, Mark. *Nathaniel Hawthorne*. New York: William Sloane Associates Inc., 1949.

Vickery, John B. "The Golden Bough at Merry Mount," *Nineteenth-Century Fiction*, XII (1957), 203–14.

Voigt, Gilbert P. "The Meaning of 'The Minister's Black Veil,' " *College English*, XIII (1952), 337–38.

Von Abele, Rudolph. "Baby and Butterfly," *Kenyon Review*, xv (1953), 280–92.

———. *The Death of the Artist: A Study of Hawthorne's Disintegration*. The Hague: Martinus Nijhoff, 1955.

Wagenknecht, Edward C. *Nathaniel Hawthorne: Man and Writer*. New York: Oxford University Press, 1961.

Waggoner, Hyatt H. *Hawthorne: A Critical Study*. rev. ed. Cambridge, Massachusetts: The Belknap Press of Harvard University Press, 1963.

Walcutt, Charles Child. " 'The Scarlet Letter' and Its Modern Critics," *Nineteenth-Century Fiction*, VII (1953), 251–64.

Walsh, Thomas F. Jr. "Hawthorne: Mr. Hooper's 'Affable Weakness,' " *Modern Language Notes*, LXXIV (1959), 404–406.

———. "Rappaccini's Literary Gardens," *Emerson Society Quarterly*, No. 19 (1960), 9–13.

———. "The Bedeviling of Young Goodman Brown," *Modern Language Quarterly*, XIX (1958), 331–36.

———. " 'Wakefield' and Hawthorne's Illustrated Ideas: A Study in Form," *Emerson Society Quarterly*, No. 25 (1961), 29–35.

Waples, Dorothy. "Suggestions for Interpreting *The Marble Faun*," *American Literature*, XIII (1941), 224–39.

Warfel, Harry R. "Metaphysical Ideas in *The Scarlet Letter*," *College English*, XXIV (1963), 421–25.

Wellborn, Grace Pleasant. "The Mystic Seven in *The Scarlet Letter*," *South Central Bulletin*, xxi, iv (1961), 23–31.

Wheeler, Otis B. "Hawthorne and the Fiction of Sensibility," *Nineteenth-Century Fiction*, xix (1964), 159–70.

Woodberry, George Edward. *Nathaniel Hawthorne*. Boston and New York: Houghton Mifflin, 1903.

Young, Philip. "Hawthorne and 100 Years: A Report from the Academy," *Kenyon Review*, xxvii (1965), 215–32.

Ziff, Larzer. "The Ethical Dimension of 'The Custom House,'" *Modern Language Notes*, lxxiii (1958), 338–44.

Zivkovic, Peter D. "The Evil of the Isolated Intellect: Hilda, in *The Marble Faun*." *Personalist*, xliii (1962), 202–13.

INDEX